OUT OF SIGHT

Steve Humphries & Pamela Gordon
OUT OF SIGHT

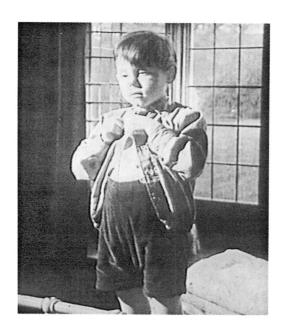

The Experience
of Disability 1900–1950

NH

NORTHCOTE HOUSE

With love to my dear parents,
Majorie and Jim Humphries
Steve Humphries

With love to Mum and Dad,
Patricia and Alan Williams
Pamela Gordon

British Library Cataloguing-in-Publication Data

A catalogue record for this book is
available from the British Library

ISBN 0 7463 0642 3

© Steve Humphries & Pamela Gordon 1992

First published in 1992 by Northcote House Publishers Ltd,
Plymbridge House, Estover, Plymouth PL6 7PZ, United Kingdom.
Tel: (0752) 705251; Fax (0752) 695699

Designed by Michael Head

Typeset by Kestrel Data, Exeter

Printed and bound in Great Britain by
The Cromwell Press, Melksham

CONTENTS

PICTURE ACKNOWLEDGEMENTS

We would like to thank the following for permission to reproduce the photographs and illustrations in this book.

Author's Collection (73), Barnardo Film Library (98), Mary Baker (131, 149, 151), Beamish Open Air Museum (14), Hazel and Dennis Boucher (147), The Boys' and Girls' Welfare Society (61), The British Council (8, 62, 76), The Children's Society (71), Julie Durham (70, 105), Cynthia Evans (130, 134), The Galton Institute (100, 136), Louis Goldberg (124), Greater London Photograph Library (15, 63, 65, 67, 79, 83, 120, 121), Hulton Picture Library (58, 118, 127), Huntley Archives (127), Marie Hagger (29, 111, 148, 149), Marjorie Jacques (97, 113), Mary Evans Picture Library (24), Ron Moore (125), National Film Archive (8, 38, 43, 62, 76), The North West Film Archive at Manchester Polytechnic (61), Pathé (18, 30, 75, 109, 117, 135), Popperfoto (17, 34), Maggie Potts (89, 101, 139), The Scottish Archive (48, 78), David and Irene Swift (114, 115, 145, 146, 150), The Trefoil Centre (48, 78), Topham (*front cover*, 13), The Wellcome Trust (100, 136), Wessex Film and Sound Archive (130, 134), Ernest Williams (21, 51), Ted and Ivy Williams (153).

ACKNOWLEDGEMENTS

We would like to thank all those who have helped us in writing this book. Special thanks to Mike Oliver, Michael Barrett, Marjorie Bartlett and Jane Campbell for their advice and perceptive comments as series consultants. We are indebted to Sue Shephard of Channel Four for her advice and support for the television series which this book accompanies.

We would also like to thank Action for Blind People, Age Concern, Arthritis and Rheumatism Council, BAHOH, BDA, Beacon Centre for the Blind, Birmingham Institute for the Deaf, Helen Bowman, Margaret Bradbury, Brighton Society for the Blind, Bristol Age Care, British Amputee Sports Association, British Blind Sports, British Council of Organisations of Disabled People, British Polio Fellowship, British Wheelchair Sports Foundation, Brittle Bones Society, Bromley Association for People with Handicaps, Central Council for the Disabled, Cerebral Palsy Helpline, Christopher Grange Centre, CHSA, the Coalitions of Disabled People, Cornwall Deaf Centre, Crown Centre for the Hard of Hearing, DBC, DIAL, Disability Action, Disability Alliance, Disability Information Service, Disabled Christians Fellowship, Disabled Drivers Association, Disablement Association in Barnet, Doncaster Residential School for the Deaf, Bob Duncan and Listening Eye, Julie Durham and Halliwick College, Edinburgh Cripple Aid Society, Elderly Accommodation Council, Keith Fieldhouse and the Disabled Miners' Centre, Freidreich's Ataxia Group, Gift of Thomas Pocklington, GLAD, Guardian Centre for the Blind, Havering Association for the Handicapped, Hertfordshire Association for the Disabled, Hi-Kent Association, Huddersfield Society for the Blind, Invalids at Home, Bob and Jenny Keenen, Keep Able, Leeds Deaf Centre, Leonard Cheshire Foundation, Lewisham Association of People with Disabilities, Macular Disease Society, MENCAP, Merseyside Society for the Deaf, Middlesex League for the Hard of Hearing, Midland Spastics Association, MIND, MS Society, NALD, National Benevolent Fund for the Aged, National Deaf-Blind League, National Federation for the Blind, NLBD, Northamptonshire and Rutland Mission to the Deaf, Northern Ireland Council on Disability, Open University, Pensioners' Link, PHAB Club, Roy Porter, Maggie Potts, Preston and North Lancashire Blind Welfare Society, Projects for the Blind, RAD, RADAR, Redbridge Association for Handicapped People, RNIB, RNID, Royal Leicestershire Society for the Blind, Royal London Society for the Blind, Royal National Throat, Nose and Ear Hospital, Royal Surgical Aid Society, Sefton Association for the Deaf, Sense, SHAPE, Sheffield Institute for the Blind, Somerset Care Limited, The Spastics Society, Spina Bifida Association, Spinal Injuries Association, SPOD, Staffordshire Society for the Deaf, Star and Garter Home, Syne Hills Home, Tapton Mount School for Visually Impaired Children, Tayside and District Deaf Centre, Tunbridge Wells Blind Welfare Committee, Visually Impaired Self-employed People's Association, Wales Council for the Disabled, Welsh Paraplegic and Tetraplegic Sports Association, Wigan and District Society for the Blind, Wolverhampton and District Institute for the Blind and all the other organisations and voluntary groups who have helped us along the way.

Thanks also to Dee Bourne, Tony Brown, Maggi Cook, Harold Frayman, Fred Hart, Steve Haskett, Mike Humphries, Joanna Mack, Kate Mitchell, Mary Morris, Patricia Potts and Alex Thompson for their own contributions towards the book and the series, and at Channel Four, Ann Pointon and Godfrey Thorpe, who have given us much assistance with the organisation of the series.

Finally, we are indebted to all the people who have shared their memories with us over the course of this project. We could not have written this book without them.

Blind children in an institution in the 1920s. Between the 1900s and the 1950s the great majority of physically disabled people in Britain were children.

INTRODUCTION

The experience of physical disability in Britain during the first half of the century is almost completely undocumented. We have little idea how it felt to be officially classified as blind, deaf or crippled and be brought up in the harsh Dickensian institutions and special schools where so many children were sent. We know even less about how the great mass of disabled children who escaped an institutional upbringing coped at home, in hospital, at school and in the streets. In an age before the emergence of the welfare state there was very little special provision for them apart from a few charity handouts. The entry of young disabled people into a world of work which often failed to recognise even their most basic needs and wants has also been largely ignored. Many were rejected by employers and forced to join the ranks of the unemployed. They often ended up living on the breadline with their families in the city slums. During the Second World War however there was a dramatic but temporary change in the economic fortune of disabled people – an extraordinary story which has never been properly documented. More than a quarter of a million were recruited into full time employment – often into skilled and responsible positions – to do jobs vacated by those who had joined the armed forces.

The most uncharted territory of all however, is the sexual identity and experience of disabled people. Until recently this has been a completely taboo subject. The denial that disabled people have sexual feelings is part of a broader denial by the able-bodied of the whole experience of disability. People with disabilities, whether they lived their lives inside or outside institutions, have remained invisible.

The aim of this book – and the television series it accompanies – is to begin to fill this important gap in our social history, by providing the first ever account of the lives of men and woman who are physically disabled. It contrasts sharply with much that has been written about physical disability in the twentieth century. There is a voluminous medical history which concentrates on the diagnosis and treatment of various disabilities. There are official histories which celebrate the 'good works' of the many charities directed at disabled people. And there are sociological studies which look critically at the functions of institutions where disabled children and adults were sent. But there has been no serious attempt to allow disabled people who grew up in the first half of the century to speak about attitudes towards them, about their hopes and fears, their ambitions, their loves, their disappointments and their struggles. Apart from a handful of biographies and autobiographies – usually of those who achieved international recognition and acclaim like

Helen Keller – there has been virtually no interest at all in the actual experience of disabled people.

This book takes a quite different focus. It looks at the lives of 'ordinary' disabled people. It portrays their lives, through their own eyes and in their own words, from childhood to adulthood. Their stories provide us with an extraordinary insight into the harsh and patronising attitudes towards disabled people in Britain between the 1900s and the 1950s. Some found it difficult or impossible to challenge the prejudice and pressure they faced at home, at school, at work, in hospitals and in institutions. The fear and shame that surrounded disability were as a result often internalised by disabled people themselves. Nevertheless most disabled people were not simply passive victims. Much of the testimony in this book reveals varying degrees of resistance to discrimination and unfair treatment. Some were determined to lead a dignified and independent life. Every day they would struggle to achieve this despite hostile and uncaring attitudes towards them. And a few were provoked into political action mounting sit-ins, strikes and demonstrations that demanded the basic rights that were so often denied to disabled people.

We began the research for the book and the television series by contacting the many voluntary organisations that represent and provide for disabled people. They gave us invaluable assistance in tracing potential interviewees born before the last war. We also wrote letters to almost every local newspaper in Britain asking for the memories of older disabled people. The response to our call for people's memories was overwhelming. We received more than a thousand letters and phone calls from people who desperately wanted to tell their stories. Nobody it seems had asked them before. For there remains a taboo on talking about disability, especially amongst the older generation. It seems to arouse strong feelings of embarrassment, fear and even disgust amongst the able-bodied. The effect of these attitudes has been to deprive disabled people of their own history.

This book tries to contribute to the re-writing of the history of disabled people from their own point of view. We the authors are both able-bodied, but the bulk of the book is devoted to the memories that we have collected from disabled men and women. The voices heard in the book are those of around fifty who originally contacted us and whom we interviewed in depth. Some of these interviews were filmed for use in the television series. Those we interviewed ranged in age between their mid-fifties and their eighties. We chose them to reflect a broad spectrum of experience in terms of different disabilities. Also we chose them because they had particularly vivid and fascinating memories. By drawing on this material we have tried to provide an authentic view of the experience of disability in Britain between the 1900s and the 1950s.

CHAPTER ONE

F<u>A</u>MILY L<u>I</u>FE

David Swift was born in 1936, the son of a miner. He was brought up with his two elder brothers and sister on a council estate on the outskirts of Nottingham. In many ways he was very similar to the other boys on the estate. He collected cigarette cards, he read the *Hotspur* comic, he kept rabbits, he was a passionate Notts County supporter and he loved swinging through the trees pretending he was Tarzan. But in one important respect David was very different from most of the other children. From birth he had an hereditary muscular disease. As a result he walked with a pronounced limp and he found it increasingly difficult to co-ordinate his finger and thumb movements. This disability meant that David quickly became an outsider. He was often treated as a lesser being or even a freak by his family. Being a sensitive boy he came to believe that his life was under threat and that he might be taken away and killed because of his disability. His entire childhood was haunted by this nagging fear of death.

My grandma used to say that I'd been cursed and that I was being punished by God for what I'd done in a past life. That was why I was disabled she said, and when I'd served out this punishment everything would be all right. I used to wonder what it was I'd done so bad to make me like this. I felt as if, well, if I'm cursed I ought to be aware of why, didn't I? But I had no idea what it could be. Nobody seemed to care. Perhaps my mum and dad were trying to cope with their own lives, I don't know. But they never showed me any affection. I couldn't speak about my feelings because weakness wasn't tolerated. My dad made me hard, hard inside. He was always wanting me to be tough. He never showed me any sympathy and I never felt like there was any love for me there. I felt as though I were different, like a freak in a side show. I remember when we all used to go to Nottingham Goose Fair and they used to have side shows and all the freaks would lay there. And I always remember thinking to myself. I wonder if I should sit up there with my feet showing? You know and people pay sixpence a time, coming in and looking at my feet. There was nobody else around like me was there? There was nowhere else I could go. I used to have this great fear that they would get rid of me or put me down because I was disabled. Fathers used to take cats and drown them in the river and I used to think that's the way they would do it to me, that's the way they killed you. We had a dog called Pete and he broke his leg. So they decided to have him destroyed and I used to think, well, why destroy dogs that can walk on three legs? I thought, perhaps they put human beings down as well,

perhaps they'll destroy me, because I can't walk? I used to spend a lot
of time on my own in the graveyard. I used to ponder over all the things
that you saw on the gravestones you know. I used to think, I wonder if
God needs me more than they, I wonder if God's wanting me? I didn't
want God to want me, I was too young. I wanted to stay on this earth.
I had this constant fear that they were going to get me. I didn't want to
die.

During the first half of the century disability was surrounded by ignorance,
fear and superstition. Age old beliefs that the birth of a disabled child was a
form of divine retribution still persisted, especially amongst the older generation. Some believed that disability represented a curse on the family, God's
punishment for evil deeds committed in the past. A few were of the opinion
that children with disabilities – often those who had epileptic fits – were
possessed by the devil. This kind of myth and folklore had a long history
reaching back to ancient civilization and the early days of Christianity when
physical disability was closely associated with spiritual uncleanliness and evil.
As the power of the church and religion declined so too did the potency of
these superstitions about disability. But they survived in some families, often
provoking terrifying fears in the minds of disabled children.

Physical disability was concentrated amongst children. Between the 1900s
and the 1950s the great majority of physically disabled people in Britain were
under fourteen years of age. More than half a million boys and girls had
rickets, polio, tuberculosis, cerebral palsy, seriously impaired vision, deafness
or a host of other disabilities. Many childhood diseases that we can today
immunise against then led to disability or death. The vast majority of children
with these disabilities came from a working class background. Some whose
mothers were particularly frail and suffering from disease might often be
disabled from birth. Many thousands of children, for example, were born
with hereditary rickets, a consequence of severe dietary deficiency in the
mother. The epidemic of venereal disease which afflicted British society in the
first decades of the century also had a devastating effect on the health of the
new born. One of the most common consequences was serious visual
impairment leading to blindness. Many disabilities however were contracted
during infancy and early childhood. Poverty, bad housing, appalling sanita-
tion and lack of healthcare meant that children were extremely unhealthy and
vulnerable to a variety of diseases that would leave them disabled. In the
poorest parts of cities like London, Liverpool and Glasgow disability was a
fact of life. Many of the large families which predominated in these areas had
at least one child with a disability.

Poverty was not only the major cause of disability in childhood. It also
shaped the attitudes of many parents to their disabled children. For centuries
the poorest families had occasionally taken desperate measures to avoid the
extra burden of a disabled child. A few would kill their deformed baby,
drowning being one of the most favoured methods. Infanticide continued –

Disabled children enjoy a day trip to Hayling Island beach in 1920. During the first half of this century the majority of physically disabled people in Britain were under fourteen years of age.

though very much reduced – into the early part of our century and was again concentrated in the poorest areas.

Iris Mickleburgh was born in 1907 in Campton, Bedfordshire, the daughter of a gardener. Her parents had separated before she was born and her mother was left to try to cope on her own.

> My mother tried to get rid of me several ways, tried to push my pram in the river but a farmer stopped her. Another time she was going to give me some tablets but grandad caught her. Left me on my own on my granny's doorstep in the end. My granny used to tell me about my mum. I only saw her a couple of times after she left me. She didn't want me 'cos I couldn't see.

Sometimes midwives and doctors conspired to kill deformed babies immediately after the birth. Often the mother had little or no knowledge of what was happening. Marjorie Collins was born in 1929 in Wimborne, Dorset. She had cerebral palsy.

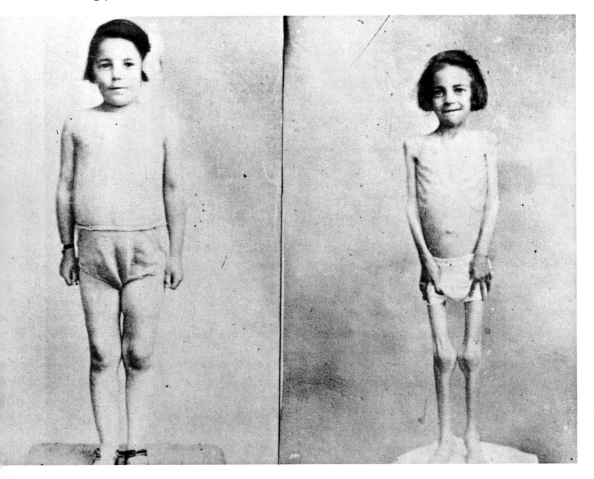

A young girl in the 1920s with rickets photographed before and after her treatment at a children's hospital. Many children were born with hereditary rickets, often a consequence of severe dietary deficiency in the mother.

My mother told me that my birth was like a nightmare to her. After hours of struggling I was eventually born, literally pulled through an iron bedstead. Mother almost lost her life through it. I was twelve pounds because they had left her pregnant for ten whole months. Apparently I was not a pretty sight from being rather bruised, with one eye pushed up into my head, which quickly righted itself. The doctor took me downstairs, put me to one side and left me for dead. But my grandma was there. She told me that she noticed that I was not breathing very well so she warmed me, washed me and put something around me and put me next to the fire. The doctor came down after seeing to my mother. He said, 'Shall I take it away, the dead baby? You don't want it left here do you?' My grandma was horrified and she said that I had to live. The doctor left without another word.

A much more common way that poor parents dealt with the problem of a disabled son or daughter was to put them into an institution where they would be brought up at little or no cost to the family. Some mothers would leave their disabled infants in the street or at the doors of the local workhouse or children's home in the hope that they would be brought up at the cost of the parish as an orphan. More often they would agree for their child to be placed in one of the many live-in institutions for 'crippled', 'physically defective', blind or deaf children.

But the majority of parents did not want their children to go to an institution. Most had harsh reputations and the institutional authorities were widely seen in working class communities as a law unto themselves. Once a child entered an institution the parents felt they had lost control over their son or daughter's life. Families were particularly strongly opposed to the growing tendency for the authorities to place children with physical disabilities in mental handicap hospitals.

A young girl being given an intelligence test at Drury Lane Special School in London in 1907. Parents were strongly opposed to the growing tendency for the authorities to view disabled children as ineducable and to place them in mental handicap hospitals.

Elsie Cooper was brought up in Ponders End, North London, the youngest of thirteen children. She had polio when she was just over a year old. As she grew up the authorities wanted to put her into an institution. Her father was a foundryman at the local factory and he resisted.

When I was nine the authorities where I lived wanted to send me away to a special institution. They told my dad that it was the only place I would be fit for. But my dad found out that this place was just for mentally handicapped kids. I would have to go there to live, goodness knows how long I would have been locked up there for. But anyway my dad said 'no'. He refused point blank, said I wouldn't learn anything there and that I was brighter then some of my brothers who went to the local school. It was only thanks to him sticking his heels in that I wasn't packed off there for good.

Ida Taylor was born in 1921 with cerebral palsy. She lived with her mother in Hertfordshire.

They wanted to send me to a mental place and lock me up. They kept coming to our house when I was about six or seven years old to ask me and me mum questions. They asked me easy things like me name and how many days in the week and about money and that. Me and me mum got real upset because I didn't want to go away and she didn't want them to take me. They said I should be in the mental place and it worried us a lot. What stopped it was that me mum took me to our doctor. He stopped those men coming round and told them I was no more mental than fly! They'd been on at us for about five years and it had made me mum ill with worry thinking I was going to be locked up.

Most working class parents in fact wanted to look after their disabled children themselves. They did their best to ensure that the child survived and enjoyed the best possible health. One priority was medical treatment. But in an age before the development of the welfare state the best health care and hospital treatment for children had to be paid for and was beyond the pocket of many parents. There were though a number of voluntary hospitals and infirmaries all over Britain where treatment was free – at least for the poorest families. The standard of treatment in these places, however, was sometimes very low. Nevertheless, some parents went to great lengths to ensure that their children were treated in these hospitals, and they made long and arduous journeys to get to them.

A Tyneside child in the 1930s who had his leg amputated and whom doctors said would never walk again. With the care and assistance of his parents he learnt how to walk and play from the age of two.

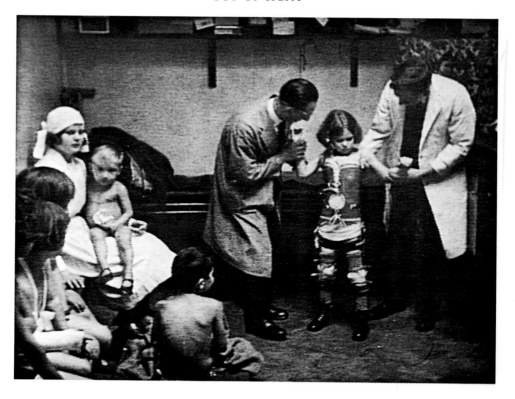

In voluntary hospitals treatment was free for poorer families. Some parents went to great lengths to ensure their children were treated in these hospitals.

Marjorie Collins remembers the immense efforts her mother made on her behalf when she was a child in the 1930s.

Mother always went out to work to earn whatever she could to get things for me. It was hard for her doing jobs like the waitressing at wedding receptions and seeing to me and my dad as well. We often had a good feed on broken wedding cake and left over sandwiches. She went scrubbing floors, cleaning other folks' homes and looking after their children, often bringing them back home, while she got her sewing machine out to earn another few pence. She would be sewing all night by gaslight sometimes. These were the many years when she had to take me around all the different hospitals and as many doctors there to try to find out what was wrong with me. Some said I had rickets, some said I was mental. She was so worried and she had no choice but to walk to the hospitals, no money for bus fares. It was often a twenty mile walk and she had to carry me. One particular day, while she was holding me under a heatray lamp at a hospital she collapsed and fainted from starvation. The doctor asked her when she had had her last meal but she couldn't remember. He gave her two shillings and sixpence to go and buy a dinner. But she was determined to find some help for me. Then at one place eight doctors took her into a little room and told her that I would never sit, stand, talk, walk and that I was blind and deaf. They drew some forms out for her to sign to put me in a home and to forget she ever had me. Mother grabbed me into her arms and cried and ran all the way home. It was so much for her to go through when at the end of it there was nothing they did to really help me.

Olive Hall, born in 1923 in South Shields, contracted polio when she was only a few months old. Her father was a teamer at the local shipyard. He and Olive's mother were determined to do the best they could for their daughter.

After I got polio my mum and dad used to carry me to hospital every day for the hot baths treatment. I had them every day for three years. But I don't think it was much good. Nothing happened. Mum and dad just tried to do anything that they could manage. There wasn't any other help for me. The big strike was on at that time so it was tough for us all. Mum used to scrub floors in a laundry to buy me proper food and to be able to keep taking me to hospital for these baths. She even pawned her engagement ring in the end, the little bit of something she had of her own. That was so I could be sent into hospital to get an operation they said would put my foot right. But it didn't work, just the opposite. I ended up with it worse. All deformed and the ankle bone all on top of the foot. My parents were trying to do their best by me but it was useless.

Gerald Turner lived in Rawmarsh, near Rotherham. He had been born with cerebral palsy in 1931.

I couldn't walk at all until I was ten and so my mum used to have to carry me everywhere or take me in an old pushchair. My parents didn't know what to do with me. Nobody ever came to help us. At home my dad had to tie me into a chair and tie my head still with a woollen scarf so they could feed me. It was all trial and error. My mum used to wheel me to the hospital every day of the week for sunray treatment and massage. That was six miles but she had no other way to try to help me. And still it didn't do any good, of course.

Surgery in voluntary hospitals and poor law infirmaries could be a terrifying experience for young disabled children. The children's fears were heightened because they were often placed in adult wards and rarely allowed to see their parents.

Christine Hollis was born in 1920, in Banbury. Her father had worked as a labourer since returning from fighting in the Great War. When she was five Christine contracted polio and was sent away from the family home in Banbury to be treated in hospital.

I had to go into hospital for some treatment and I was the only child in the ward. I was so scared and nervous especially when my parents were sent away. They didn't have visiting like they do today. I saw things in there that no child should have to see and it affected me for years. Old really sick people, people having to swallow tubes down and being in pain. When it came time to have my operation the nurse said that I was going down to the theatre to see Charlie Chaplin. But of course it was the operating theatre. They just clamped something over my mouth and nose. I remember struggling as they dripped the chloroform into it. It was like a nightmare and still is.

Poor parents often went through the embarrassment of begging from charities to obtain treatment or medical aids for their disabled children. Elsie Cooper:

I lay in a bath chair till I was seven because we just couldn't afford any treatment. I remember once my mother scraped together a few coppers to take me to the doctor's. She had to carry me all the way there too. But he wouldn't do anything for me without money. So mother had to try to get me some help on her own. She used to go around to different charities to beg for money to buy me some callipers. They would give her a letter guaranteeing her a certain amount of money towards my callipers and boots. And we had to wait until we had enough letters to make up the cost. But she practically had to go down on her knees to them. The church charities were especially strict. They just turned you away if you didn't attend their particular church every week. Otherwise they didn't want to know.

Many working class parents could not afford the special foods and improved diet that hospitals and doctors often recommended for children with disabilities. To get them some parents and their children had to go through constant means tests. For some mothers however the humiliation of these rituals was too much to bear.

When Anne Klein was six years old in 1931 she was run over by a baker's van. The injury became worse over the following year until finally TB developed in her legs. Anne spent much of that time in hospital. In 1932 she was discharged and went home to the East End of London to live with her widowed mother and four brothers and sisters. Her mother's main source of income was the public relief fund.

When I left hospital I would have been about seven. The doctors told my mother that I had to have lots of fresh fruit and veg and nutritious food to build my strength up. 'Course we didn't have the money. Bread and dripping was often the tea in our house in those days. So my mum had to take me to a special tribunal. I've got a picture in my mind of a lot of big fat men sitting at a long table and little me sitting on a chair in front of them all on my own. They were deciding whether they would let me have anything extra. My mum was so nervous because she knew that without that money I would probably get ill again. I was granted ten shillings a week only and they said if I wanted it kept up then we had to go back every week and go through the whole system again. But it was so humiliating begging for this money that we couldn't face it the next week. It had upset my mum and she said we weren't going again. So we had to manage without the extra. It was a very hard time for us all.

Extra food could sometimes be obtained from charity handouts but any assistance for children with severely impaired vision was much more difficult to obtain. Eye tests and spectacles for the children usually had to be paid for privately and could be very expensive. Often parents saved up for one pair of spectacles but if they were lost or broken, or if the lenses needed strengthening, or if the spectacle frames became too small, they were too costly to replace. One pair of spectacles sometimes had to last for an entire childhood. However for children with the most severely impaired vision, wearing spectacles made virtually no difference to their sight anyway.

Ernest Williams was born in 1915, the son of an agricultural labourer who eked out a living for his family in the village of Much Cowarne in Herefordshire.

Ernest Williams (far right) pictured with his brother and sister in 1922. The family lived on the breadline and even though Ernest had severely impaired vision they could not afford to replace his broken spectacles.

Being the blind boy I came in for a fair amount of – not exactly spoiling – but certainly as good treatment as was available. Extra spoonful of honey going to bed, for example, when honey was available. I suppose I got preferential treatment from my mother. I do recall that if I used to be ill she'd be very concerned about it. She would gather me up to her, shedding a few tears over me and one got a lot of comfort out of that, of course. But poverty was one of our day to day experiences. One had a resignation to the fact that even if there were things that could be done like having spectacles one didn't press these things. In my time not many children did have spectacles. Certainly I knew that they cost money. I had a pair once that my mother had got for me and I broke them or lost the lens and I was very concerned going home having to admit this. I didn't expect anything to be done about it because of the cost. It cost more money to buy spectacles than to buy a pair of shoes. And that was relevant in those days. So my spectacles couldn't be replaced. The main concern was for the business of living.

Even a visit to the doctor was too costly for some families. Under the National Insurance Scheme fathers were often the only member of the family entitled to free health care. Even as late as the 1930s disabled children were widely treated with folk medicines and quack cures to avoid the expense of paying for the doctor. Most children – who observed the shortage of money in the family – simply accepted that this was their lot.

Marie Hagger was brought up in Tottenham, North London before the last war, the daughter of a railway porter. She had severely impaired hearing.

My mother and father did love me. How can I describe it? It was just a sign of the times. In them days there was no money about. So at the first suggestion from anyone that you ought to see a doctor resulted in hands thrown up in the air in horror. It was four shillings and sixpence to see a doctor. They hadn't got it. It wasn't a question of, 'Oh please find it for me.' They couldn't. So you didn't even think about it. So whether you were deaf or you'd got a bad arm, bad leg or whatever, a home cure was the only result. It was all you could expect. All sorts of things, except the right thing, that was get the correct treatment. No, they never did because they couldn't afford to. So my deafness didn't have a hope, no hope in getting any treatment at all.

Folk medicines and patent cures often varied from one area to another. They were part of the folk wisdom of the working class community passed on from one generation to the next. In practically every street there would be neighbours eager to give advice and assistance to a family with a disabled child.

Hilda Donnelly was born in 1914 in Hartlepool. Her father was fighting in the First World War and so when Hilda contracted polio at the age of one and a half her mother had to cope alone with only the help of her neighbours.

When I got polio I was really ill and my mum had to get the doctor out to me. He came and said what I had but then he never seemed to bother after that. Mum couldn't afford to send me into hospital and so the doctor left it up to her to care for me. I remember screaming whenever the bedclothes touched my legs at first. She was so worried about me. But all our neighbours were very kind. They all had remedies that they told mum to try on me. Anything that might make me even a little better, I got. She gave me Dr Castle's tablets, they were a health tonic. I took them for years. I got Scotts Emulsion from one woman in the street. Another man used to bring two buckets of sea-water up from the shore every morning. Mum would heat it up and bath me in that. Then they massaged my legs and back with olive oil. She tried absolutely everything to make me walk again.

As well as trying to cure their children lots of parents did their best to make a disabled son or daughter more mobile. Callipers, crutches and wheelchairs were all expensive items that many families could not afford. So they often made their own DIY versions out of what materials were available.

Alice Maguire, born in 1909 in Croxton, Norfolk, had polio when she was eight. Her father had just returned from fighting in the war and her parents were trying to set up a small shop in the village.

When I got polio it was during the First World War. The doctor thought it was rheumatism, until they noticed my leg had started to wither away. But they didn't want to know at the hospital. They were busy with the war so there was no bed for me. It was my mother who looked after me. She massaged my legs three times a day until they were a bit stronger. Then she used to stand behind me with her arms under my armpits and walk me along the floor. She used to push me to school every day with me sitting on her bike so I wouldn't have to be at home all day. I was learning to walk again but my bad leg wouldn't support me. My great-grandfather was the village blacksmith so mother asked him to make me a special iron support for the leg. It was like a home-made calliper with leather straps to hold it onto my leg. After that I could walk much better. And the kids in our village used to get me to strike sparks on the road with my iron as we walked along to school.

Eva Shackleton was born in 1920 in Armley, Leeds. When she was four she fell down the stairs at home. She damaged her leg very badly and TB developed. The leg was amputated a few months later.

After my accident I couldn't get around except for hopping around or on my bottom. I used to want to go off and play with the others but I couldn't very well crawl along the street outside. I never had a wheelchair or even a pushchair because then people just couldn't afford to buy one.

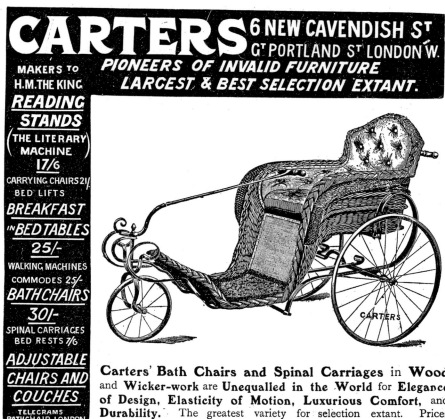
Carters' Bath Chairs and Spinal Carriages in Wood and Wicker-work are Unequalled in the World for Elegance of Design, Elasticity of Motion, Luxurious Comfort, and Durability. The greatest variety for selection extant. Prices from **30/-**.

Write for Catalogue, 600 Illustrations, Post Free.

Wheelchairs were very expensive and beyond the pockets of most families. Poorer parents often made their own DIY versions out of scrap materials in an effort to make their disabled child more mobile.

There was nobody who could help us out. One day my dad got two old broom handles and made them into crutches for me. He put padding over the top for under my arms and cut them to my height so then I could practice up and down our street with these homemade crutches and then I could go out and play with the other children. That's how I got around for years.

Middle class parents usually had the means to pay for much better medical treatment for children with disabilities. This involved doctors, physicians, private clinics or paying for superior treatment in voluntary hospitals. The medical attention they received was much more likely to be beneficial than that which was given to poorer patients.

Betty Leach was born in 1920 in Cardiff, the daughter of a successful potter and artist. She had cerebral palsy.

They didn't have a proper name for us in those days. The doctors didn't really know what to call somebody like me. But my family was determined to get treatment for me. First of all my mother took me to the hospital in London quite a lot. We used to love coming down to London and staying there. In the day we went to do my treatment with Dr Cameron. He was very good and he taught mother how to massage my legs properly. The only trouble was that the sister in the ward was rather a dragon and mother didn't like her. She used to get very frustrated that she couldn't learn enough to help me. So she looked everywhere to get a good nurse type to come to our home and look after me. In the end we got an excellent person. It was a lady who taught all the school subjects but she was a medical gymnast as well. She came and did massage with me and special exercises. My goodness she got me on terrifically, splendid. It was hard work though, she even gave me marks for conduct. I'd never been made to try so hard in my life, but that's what I needed.

Marjorie Hughes was born with a severe congenital limb deficiency in 1920 in Risca, near Newport. Her father was a headmaster and with the financial help of his parents Marjorie was able to travel with her mother for treatment in London.

At first I was in a very nice nursing home in London. Sir Robert Jones attended to me and because I was a private patient my mother was allowed to stay with me. Without that treatment when I was so young I would have been much worse. I would never have walked if I hadn't been there and had the operations that I did. But it was very, very expensive. My grandparents used to help out financially so that I could stay there and so mother could spend all her time with me, getting me as well as they could to take me home again.

Although most families did what they could to provide material support for their disabled children, the emotional relationships they formed with them were much more complex, contradictory and sometimes damaging. The birth of a disabled child often provoked feelings of profound disappointment and even disgust in many parents. This was only partly a consequence of the extra cost and care involved in bringing up a child with special needs.

From the mid-nineteenth century onwards there had been a growing emphasis in British society on the importance of masculinity, physical strength, fitness, athleticism and sport – what has come to be termed 'Muscular Christianity'. These values were stressed in schools and in immensely in-fluential uniformed youth movements of the time like the Boy Scouts and the Boys' Brigades. It was all part of the new ideology of imperialism with its great pride in the supremacy of the British army and navy and the power of the Empire. All British citizens – however poor – could take comfort in the certain knowledge that they formed a superior race, destined to rule the waves.

Failure to live up to this mythical stereotype often caused great shame and suffering to the parents of children with disabilities. For some men the idea that they were the father of a disabled child seriously undermined their self respect and masculinity. Similarly mothers whose children were either born with a disability or who contracted a disabling disease in childhood increasingly felt that they had failed themselves, their family and their country.

For during the first decades of the century there was growing state intervention into child care with the development of clinics, regular medical inspections and mothercraft classes, all geared to improving the nation's health in the next generation. This movement brought better health care but its downside was the reinforcement of negative attitudes towards disability. Some parents were so ashamed of their disabled son or daughter, they would keep them at home, hidden from public view, and rarely took them out with the rest of the family.

Muriel Faulkner was born in 1902, the daughter of a general labourer and she contracted polio in 1904. Her family lived in the village of Bronesberrow Heath near Ledbury.

> They kept you where people couldn't see you. They kept you out of sight. After I'd had my polio my parents didn't really let me out much at all. I was never allowed to walk out with the rest of our family because of how I looked with my limp and all. Sometimes they used to take all the other children on the horse and cart to a show in another village. That was a real treat but I was never allowed to go. I was usually sent to my gran's whilst they all went off. It was as if they were ashamed of me and even as a child that made me feel awful.

Fathers often felt the shame most acutely and mothers would sometimes go to great lengths to keep disabled children out of their way. Although Marjorie Collins' mother endured great sacrifices to help her daughter, her father never wanted to see her.

> I never saw my father much when I was little. He never denied I was his child but he blamed mum for it, for how I was. She had to do everything for me and him. By the time he came in from work then he wanted me to be in bed kind of thing. He wouldn't even sit at the same table with me. I was a thorn in his flesh so I tried to keep out of his way. He thought I was a one off. He'd never met another spastic and he thought that I was something terrible.

In some families the whole subject of disability was taboo. The parents could not accept or come to terms with the fact that they had a child with a disability. By not talking about it they hoped that it might somehow go away. This approach could have traumatic and distressing consequences for the children. It all began in early childhood when the parents gave their son or daughter an entirely mythical explanation of their disability. The impression was given that they weren't really disabled at all. David Swift:

> It was all a kind of hush hush thing. They told me that I'd fallen out of a tree. Well, I had fallen out of a tree when I was seven, broke my arm and fractured my ribs. But that wasn't the cause. Anyway I started to use that as a reason because I just never knew what was wrong with me.

Joyce Budynowicz was born in 1927 in Tamworth. She had cerebral palsy but this was never discussed by her family.

> My parents told me that I had fallen out of my cot when I was little and that was why I had my disability. I believed that for years, until I was about twenty-two. I just didn't know that I'd been born like this because it was absolutely never talked about in the family. I'd fallen out of my cot and that was the reason given. They never made any allowances for me when we were children. Even though I couldn't walk properly I had to battle on. None of the family admitted any difficulty I was having because that would have been like saying out loud that I was disabled.

Margaret Bennett had cerebral palsy when she was born in 1925 in Huddersfield. Her father was a textile worker.

> In the early days it wasn't brought out into the open. Somehow or other if any child was born physically handicapped it was hushed up and kept out of the way. In my family my disability was just ignored. Mum and dad didn't tell me that I was disabled or why or anything. When I was quite little I asked my dad if the doctors had said anything when I was born, whether they had said why I was different than other children. My dad just told me that I had a bit of rheumatism. Then they didn't mention it again. They both knew the truth but they weren't telling. I didn't find out the truth about myself until I went to the doctor's on my own years later, when I was grown-up, what I had got and that I had been born with it. It was only then that I started to understand about myself.

Children in families like this who found that their sight, their hearing or their walking were seriously impaired and were getting worse, often could not talk to their parents about the problem. Many parents preferred to think that their children were slow learners rather than admit that they had a physical disability. The children themselves were also encouraged to adopt this view of themselves. This often led to confusion and immense stress. Marie Hagger:

> I soon realised that my deafness was something that I ought to be ashamed of. It was something shameful. The truth is that I couldn't talk

to anyone about my hearing. I tried many times to broach the subject, to say that I was going deaf. I tried to talk to my father on one occasion and he said, 'Don't talk to me about that, you have to get on with your life and that's that.' My mother was a happy woman. All she wanted to do was to laugh so she didn't like to see me miserable at all. Even though she realised that my hearing was not quite right she still thought I was a little bit backward, not as bright as the others. She preferred to think that. Sometimes she would look at me and she must have seen that far away look in my eyes and she would say, 'You can't do anything about it. We've all got something wrong with us.' I thought to myself, I'm wasting my time even talking about it. They don't want to know and they can offer nothing to advise or comfort or to counsel. There was nothing to be done and after that my mother didn't talk about it, my father downright refused to comment on it at all. In fact the whole subject was taboo.

An even more disturbing feature of the refusal to accept a child's disability was the use of brutal methods to try to cure it. David Swift:

One night my dad was coming home from the pub and he got run over and broke his leg. The hospital gave him two sticks. And after he'd been using them for some time and he didn't need them anymore I started to use them. I found that I could walk around better with the sticks and he saw me doing it. He says, 'Give me those sticks here. Give 'em here, you're not having them.' He took them off me because they highlighted my disability. He was a hard man. I don't know whether he was trying to make me walk without sticks, but they were such a comfort to me. I felt that I could have got through life better with them. When my legs were getting worse my dad said I was walking like a drunken man. And I said I couldn't do anything to change that. So he made me sit on the sofa and he says, 'Right, straighten your feet.' And I'm sitting there trying to straighten them. I told him that I couldn't and he got really angry, kept shouting, 'Straighten them, put your legs together!' and hitting my legs, beating them. I think he were trying to shock me into doing it 'cos he thought my disability was something in my mind.

Some fathers put their disabled sons through punishing fitness routines, a reflection of the great concern with physical strength and masculinity in the early part of the century. Louis Goldberg was born with cerebral palsy in Stepney, East London in 1916. When he was five the family moved to Brighton where his father started his own garage.

When the doctor saw me, when I was about two, he said that my parents should just sit me in a corner and more or less forget about me because there was nothing he could do for me. But my dad was determined to

Marie Hagger (right) pictured in 1936 at the age of 13. Despite her increasingly impaired hearing Marie's greatest love was tap dancing.

Marie's father (above) was a First World War veteran who worked as a railway porter on the LNER. Her mother (right) was a full time housewife. They both refused to talk about Marie's deafness and the whole subject became taboo within the family.

treat me the same as my two brothers. They were A1, very fit. And dad was solid muscle, eighteen stone and very keen on the Huckenschmidt fitness methods. He was a Russian, a big burly man who did an exercise and fitness regime that was really popular in the twenties. Every morning my dad had my brothers and me sponging down in freezing cold water then doing lots of different exercises, running and so on. But for a spastic, that's a way of killing him. The cold water used to make me go into awful spasms. I did what I could to keep up with my brothers. I was only young so I couldn't do much else. But I hated it. It was something horrible that I had to try to do.

David Swift came from a family and a neighbourhood famous for its boxing prowess. As a result of this he had to endure appallingly violent treatment, supposedly designed to 'cure' his disability.

My dad always wanted me to be a boxer like me other brothers and me cousin. He always had us shadow boxing against the wall, hitting the wall. But walls don't hit you back do they? It's when people started hitting you back. It's all right learning how to throw a punch if nobody's

Sparring at a boys' gymnasium in the 1940s. A few parents of disabled boys forced them to box in the hope that it might provide a shock cure for their disability.

punching back. But my Uncle Joe had a boxing gymnasium where all the boxers went to train. Well, my dad said he was going to take me to my Uncle Joe's to straighten my legs out. They put me on this couch and gave me some sunray treatment on my legs and warmed 'em all up. Then they started massaging them and manipulating them, trying to get them straight. Then he says, 'Right, now, start punching the bag.' As the weeks went by and people saw me punching this bag and they must have thought I looked quite healthy. Next thing I know, I'm in the ring and there's boxers all punching me round. Kept hitting me in the jaw. And when you get hit in the jaw it seems as if they are knocking your brain out. And I couldn't move out of the way. I just had to try to cover myself up from all the blows. I couldn't box. There was no co-ordination, you know. I'd be swinging around wildly with my hands you know, with the gloves. I liked the gloves because they couldn't see my hands inside them but boxing was hopeless. And you'd come out and feel humiliated. The other lads used to say, 'You're not so tough now are you Swifty.' And they'd jeer at you. But I didn't say, 'Well, look at the advantages you've got. You've got your hands, you've got your legs.' I didn't say that. Why didn't I turn around and say that? Why didn't I give it to them? I let 'em treat me like shit. But you didn't complain. You couldn't complain to my dad. You just had to take it. And I'm coming home with all cuts and bruises. But my dad never said anything. Violence never bothered my dad. It was hard for me to survive in that kind of environment.

The parent's refusal to accept the disability was often passed onto their children. A disabled son or daughter often internalised similar feelings of shame, anxiety and fear that were experienced by their parents. However, this stigma was often more intense for them because it was coupled with a strong feeling of guilt. It was they who actually had the disability so it seemed that all the heartache that resulted was their fault. Many felt that they had inflicted a terrible disaster on their families, just by virtue of their existence. To compensate for this, children with disabilities often made special efforts to cause as few problems as possible for their parents. Ernest Williams:

I realised at a young age that it was important for me to have a way of ensuring that I knew where things were in our cottage, not least because breaking things, of course, was quite a serious matter. The cottage was very dark, there weren't enough windows. If you broke a cup or saucer, it wasn't just a matter of getting another one out. Frequently there were only as many as one needed for the family. And it meant a trip into Hereford to buy others. Preserving what one had was essential. Now, I used to ensure that I knew where absolutely everything was. I had to get at things without having to hunt for them and I did that by simply knowing where I could find them. I always put my boots and socks in a specific place, whereas my sisters would probably pull theirs off and put them under the kitchen table. But I always had a specific place for putting all my things and there was always a difficulty if they weren't where I expected them to be. Chairs and the chest of drawers, and a bench against the wall. These things were very much in my own mind, I didn't have to look. They were there. I remember breaking a lamp glass by bringing in a stick we were going to break up to put on the fire. And I turned round with it and hit the lamp glass and smashed it and – oh dear! And we had to wait until Saturday when we could buy another lamp glass in Hereford. That meant candles. It was as simple as that. So care in not breaking things was very much the order – the way of life.

It was unusual at this time for boys to make any real contribution to the many domestic chores that needed to be done around the home. This was thought to be women's work and was normally done by mothers and daughters. Boys with disabilities were often so keen to please their parents they would break through these deep rooted gender divisions.

Kenneth Matthews was born in Swansea in 1923 and contracted polio in 1924 which left his arms particularly disabled.

I used to go on all kinds of errands for my grandma especially. I lived with her and I used to do as much as I could to make myself useful. I carried heavy buckets of coal in from the shed and lots of jobs like that. I helped her around the house as well as I could. It was because I felt in my mind that I was a second class citizen, that I wasn't as good as the next lad. I felt that even when I was young I had to do that much extra, push myself a bit hard like.

Some children felt so threatened and insecure, they believed that they were living under a constant threat of forcible death because of their disability. For boys like this domestic labour took on an even greater psychological importance. David Swift:

I seemed to be always trying to earn my right to live, you know. I was a good boy to my mum and dad. I used to clean up for them, I used to cook, do errands. I used to do all the chores. My dad was a miner and used to get all coal in the house so I would clear it up. I used to go and clean the bedrooms as best I could, make all the fires, get up and look after my baby brother. I did everything I could for my mum and especially when my dad came home, then I would dig the garden for him or go to the shops on my soap box. I even stayed in the kitchen while my mum had a miscarriage and looked after her for fourteen days while she was in bed. Anything to please them, to make me seem worthwhile being there. I used to want to do all these things. I was inasmuch saying, 'I am useful, I am doing something, don't forget me.' You know, I used to have to earn my life.

Children with feelings of insecurity and inferiority as deep as these experienced a terrible sense of isolation and loneliness. Some, like David, looked – at least briefly – to religion as a source of comfort and hope.

You never cried, you weren't allowed to do that. So I never let it show, how upset I was. I used to go to the graveyard near our house and sit down there on my own. I sat down on one of the gravestones and looked down at my legs and prayed for them to be straight when I woke up next morning. I used to wish and wish for God to make me like everybody else. I'd speak to this God in earnest and say to him to please make my legs so that I could walk like other people. I couldn't understand if this God was so loving like my grandma told me he was, why me? And why did I never get any answers from him?

The pent up emotions inside these children was occasionally released in acts of domestic violence. Usually their anger was directed against members of their family and the homes in which they lived. Marie Hagger:

I used to get angry at times because of the frustrations. And to overcome these frustrations sometimes you have to let your hair down, as they say, be yourself. Several times with my parents being so complacent and seemingly uncaring about me I just wanted to do something to stir things up, I think for good reason too. I think my hearing would have been enough to bring it out in anyone. Well, it did in me. One day in my frustration I looked at the Welsh dresser in our kitchen. I picked up cup by cup and plate by plate and simply smashed the lot on the ground. At that time there was lino on the floor so there was no hope of recovery. There wasn't a plate or a cup left unbroken. After I'd done it I looked on the floor – I was absolutely petrified. And I had a feeling of elation at the same time. I felt elated. I felt I'd achieved something not nice and good because my deafness is not nice and nobody else likes it either. Well it's about time I showed that it's not nice and I agree with them one hundred per cent. So what can I do about it? Smash all the crockery up and see what that did. Of course it didn't do anything at all. My sister was horrified, 'You'll cop it now, you'll get it now, you wait.' Well I waited and nothing much happened. I think my mother might have told me off but there was all the broken crockery, I thought she'd have gone mad. No, no. I don't think my father ever knew. I think it was covered up and something else was bunged up on the shelves. That was the end of it. But it gave me the feeling to exert myself and get rid of some of the build-up that was going on inside me. The build-up inside me was tremendous. It was like an unexploded bomb. All the time. And some time or another it was going to go off.

CHAPTER TWO

A CHILD APART

Every morning when Marie Hagger set off for school in Tottenham, North London, in the 1930s she felt sick with fear and apprehension. From the time she began school her hearing deteriorated rapidly. Every day she knew she would be straining to make sense of conversations, instructions and lessons that she could not hear. In the classroom, in the playground and in the street she would be desperately guessing and lip-reading to try to understand the increasingly silent world around her. Her worst fear was that her growing deafness would be exposed and she would be publicly humiliated, taken away from home and put into an institution. Even though Marie's deafness was a taboo subject at home, family life at least provided her with some love and security. In contrast, the world outside seemed a very cold, hostile and threatening place. Her struggle to survive in it and to keep her secret was a very private one. She felt totally alone.

I never admitted that I was deaf to the other children. We played the same sort of games as everyone. If I missed a word here and there, being young, nobody particularly noticed. If you're playing certain games and you play it wrong nobody is going to come up to you and say, 'You did that wrong.' They weren't really interested. And obviously, sometimes it would be to their advantage. If I lost, they could win. And that's what often happened. When it came to choosing sides, though, I would find that I was often left out. But I just tried to be accepted. It never entered my head to tell them that I was deaf because somewhere in the back of my mind I had a terrible fear that had I told them, they would have totally rejected me, they would have looked at me like I was something from outer space and I would be forgotten in their games. The fact was that I wasn't holding my own but I just hoped and prayed that the school and the other children wouldn't realise it. I became very sensitive as a child. And I was absolutely petrified of sticking out so much that I would be sent to an institution. My fears about that were uppermost in my mind. I think that aspect alone drove me almost to the verge of doing something terrible. I couldn't imagine anything worse than going to an institution. I thought I'd never be able to come home. The more I thought about it, I thought if I died I'd be happier never knowing any of this terrible pain. I found it hard – the isolation – all the harder to bear. The loneliness as well. Although I had other children, surrounded by other

Most disabled children from a working class background were encouraged to go out and play on the streets.

children, I felt this terrible isolation and loneliness because I realised I was not part of their world wholly, not entirely. At school I looked at the whole class because I was different and I said to myself, I don't belong to any of you. I haven't got what you lot have all got. I'm lacking in some way. I'm not full, I'm not a fully made person. I started to think of myself as an anonymity really, more than anything else. Looking at the world, looking at the school, looking at everything as though I was on the sideline, on the touchline. And that's how I was beginning to view the world. I didn't feel part of it any more. I felt apart from it, not a part. That's when my problem became very, very big – almost insurmountable. Almost something that I couldn't cope with. I often wondered how far I could go with my hearing before something went. I honestly believed my ears would one day explode. That's how I thought as a child, I mean. I thought they would burst one day. Finished, like a candle going out or a match.

For most children with disabilities life outside the home and the immediate family was fraught with difficulties and dangers. Most families provided them with some degree of protection, but when removed from this they were highly vulnerable. They were especially vulnerable in the rough and tumble world of children's play.

Before the last war streets, fields and public parks were the main play areas for working class children. Children spent much of their free time playing outside as most homes were so cramped and overcrowded there was little space for them indoors. Although some parents tried to hide their disabled children away, most encouraged them to go out to play on the streets, if only to enjoy some peace and privacy themselves in the evenings. This could be a very harrowing time for children with disabilities for many working class streets were dominated by gangs of various ages that were highly physical and aggressive. They were also very conformist and frequently victimised children who were seen as different in any way. To avoid being rejected as an outsider a child – especially a boy – had to be a member of the street gang and to join in the same activities as the other children. This commonly involved many 'dares', tests of courage and territorial street fights with rival gangs from neighbouring streets.

David Swift did everything he could to be accepted in his street gang on the council estate where he lived in Nottingham in the 1940s. But the disability in his legs often resulted in him being told off or injured.

The kids never came out with it point blank, 'Get stuffed – you're a cripple!' But they would do it in an indirect way. They'd just go off and leave me. If I couldn't do it, couldn't keep up then that was your look out. And often if I did play then I'd get into trouble. We used to tie string to people's door knockers then pull the string and run away. But I always got caught. Even when we went scrumping I got caught. Once I got stuck up the apple tree because I just couldn't get down as fast as the others. We all had gangs at that time as well and I got into a gang because my older brother was in it. We used to have raids on each others gangs. It was either Beechdale Gang or Denewood Gang and you had a dustbin lid to protect you and we used to throw bricks at each other. And of course when they used to charge I couldn't get away. I used to get battered with bricks. Then we played games like *Rum-Stick-a-Bum* and in that you had to jump onto someone's back. But I could never play that because I couldn't jump. We used to play on the stream as well and float down it on an old Anderson shelter roof. But when it got to the part of the stream where it was going to crash they'd all jump off. So consequently I used to get injured.

Disabled children who couldn't join in these kinds of activities were often seen as weak and inferior. Some would be bullied and even terrorised by gangs.

Dorothy Hadley who was blind from birth was brought up in the village of Tettenhall near Wolverhampton in the 1920s. She was constantly bullied in the streets but her family eventually found an effective way of providing her with some protection.

I used to be frightened to go out when I came home on my school holidays, I had no friends really. I was always lonely and would have loved to have had some friends to play with. The boys used to run behind me and jump on my back when I used to go out for walks. They used to pull my hair and jump out at me to scare me. They'd call me names like 'funny eyes' and so on. I'd graze my knees and it would upset me a lot; I used to be sitting there crying. So what happened? My grandfather got me an alsatian dog. I was only eight at the time, but I had this big dog, and that did the trick. She'd give a low growl and that was enough, the boys left me alone then.

Even if they escaped physical attacks most children with disabilities were frequently taunted and verbally abused by the children in their neighbourhood.

Elsie Antley was born in 1909 and brought up in Billston in the West Midlands. From birth she suffered from excess water in her legs as a result of which she had severe difficulty in walking and had to wear special boots.

I used to have to wear very high thick leather boots all the time, even in the hot weather. If I didn't my ankles would swell up so much that they would drag on the ground. These boots were right up to my calves, all done up with hooks and laces. I hated them. The children called me names and were so cruel because of how I looked in these boots. They would all be wearing sandles and so I looked out of place. If I had the chance to take them off, to escape some of their taunting, I would, but then it would be worse because my legs would all swell up.

Christine Hollis was brought up in Banbury in the 1920s. She contracted polio at the age of five which left her legs disabled.

I felt different. The others would sort of look at me. It was as if they saw me as inferior. That was how they made me feel. I wanted to join in but of course I couldn't. I tried very hard to keep up with the games but quite often I would end up sitting them out. There was one boy especially though who I used to dread seeing. He was truly horrible to me. He would walk behind me and mimic my way of walking whilst he sang *'Tiptoe Through the Tulips'* or some other kind of taunt. A lot of the children used to laugh. Every night I would go home and tell my mother what had been happening, how he had been taunting me. But she just said that he would be sorry one day so I couldn't do anything.

As most working class children tended to form group or gang friendships with strong 'tribal' loyalties to the other children in the street or neighbourhood, children with disabilities were often excluded. Some found themselves without any real friends at all. The cruellest fate was to be rejected by everyone and derided as a kind of monster or freak.

Bob Hendley was born in the mining village of Thurmscoe near Doncaster in 1918. He had polio as a young child.

A child with impaired vision pictured on the streets of London in the 1930s.
Many disabled children found themselves isolated and without any real friends.

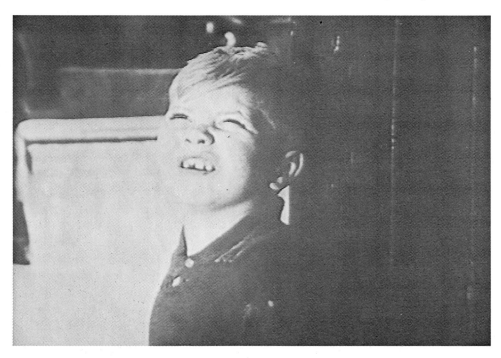

I had no friends in our village. I used to go around more on a level with the dogs because I had to cross my legs over each other and use them like a shovel to get about. I looked strange to folk I suppose. I just used to muck around on my own, down at the pit-yards amongst the coal, until the policeman caught me and took me up home again. The other kids in the village used to dare me to stand on my hands on the corner of our street. They used to laugh at me and sometimes throw me sweets. Sometimes people used to pass and throw pennies at me.

Disabled children from a middle class background often enjoyed greater protection from this brutal side of children's independent culture. Middle class children's play was normally much more home-based and adult controlled than in poorer families and this protective element was often heightened if a son or daughter was disabled. Better off parents usually did their utmost to shelter their disabled son or daughter from the harsh and aggressive attitudes of other children.

Friendships were strictly controlled by the parents and all play activities took place in the home or the garden. In the closest families the parents themselves often played the part of substitute friends, taking their disabled child out at weekends. Although children from this kind of background were spared the worst traumas that confronted most disabled children from working class homes, the life that they were forced to lead was often very narrow and frustrating. They too were isolated and alone, but in a different way.

Marjorie Hughes was born with a congenital limb deficiency in 1920. She lived in Risca, just outside Newport, with her mother and her father who was a headmaster.

Most children like to rough and tumble a lot when they play. Of course I couldn't take part in games like that. So to a certain degree I was stuck. We used to play house in our garden a bit but a lot of the time I was left out, left at home. Because I was on my own my mother bought me lots of books. I grew to love reading. I read everything but my favourite was *The Scarlet Pimpernel*. It was so exciting, full of action like. My mother took me to see the film as well when it came out. Leslie Howard as the Pimpernel. Then later I read Dickens and Robert Louis Stevenson and the Brontës. I did even write a few stories of my own as a child. Sitting so long I could let my imagination run away with myself. So most of my time was spent like that. And mother took me out for rides in the car. She was a good driver. We went into the country and all round the lanes, then into Newport shopping or just looking round the shops. It was wonderful to get out in amongst everyone. In the evenings she would take me to the concerts sometimes. I heard the Vienna Philharmonic and Paul Robeson. Those were wonderful evenings of sheer delight. If it hadn't have been for the car though, I would hardly have been out.

Sometimes my mother didn't have the time and I was left really to amuse myself as best I could. And often that could get quite lonely indeed.

Betty Leach was born with cerebral palsy in 1920 in Cardiff. Her father, who was a successful potter, and her mother tried hard to find ways of occupying Betty's time.

My mother bought me an old-fashioned typewriter so that I had something to do at home. I used to sit for hours tapping out the words and writing to lots of people. But that's all there was for me to do. Now and again someone would try to take me somewhere or play games with me but it was so difficult because I couldn't get out easily. The children around where we lived were always so active of course, running about whilst I could really only stay at my typewriter. That was the trouble and I know that I gave my mother a hard time just because I was bored. I would cry a lot and have tempers.

The main friendships formed by disabled children in working class areas were often with girls. Although girls participated in the gangs they were generally less enthusiastic than the boys. They would spend much time in smaller groups of two or three skipping, playing hopscotch or just talking. In this setting children with disabilities were likely to find more sympathy and were sometimes helped to join in.

Gladys Berry, born in Sheffield in 1912 suffered from hereditary rickets.

I could not walk at all, only shuffle on my bottom. I was under the hospital's care and they tried me with splints but they were no use, and I was in a spinal carriage flat on my back for ages. I had some friends on our street and they treated me all right. In fact, my best friends used to argue over who'd wheel me to the park, and when they were skipping in the street they used to let me turn one end of the skipping rope for them. I had a best friend, Hannah, and it was her that learnt me to walk when I was ten and I started school.

Olive Hall was brought up in South Shields and had polio when she was only one year old in 1924.

If you were disabled the other children didn't really want to know you. I never told my mother and father because that would have made them feel awful. So I had to put up with a fair amount of scoffing and taunting from the other girls and boys. It was mostly about my foot and how it looked different than theirs and how it made me walk. There was one girl who used to kind of look after me though. I've no idea why she did it. Maybe she guessed how bad I felt. She was an older girl so the others would always take notice of her if she told them to stop being horrible to me. And she used to come over and talk to me. I thought a lot of her, just for sticking up for me a bit whilst nobody else would.

Children with disabilities could often rely on able-bodied brothers and sisters for some degree of friendship and support. In particular they would often try to give a disabled member of the family some protection against bullying and verbal abuse. This occasionally led to fights and disturbances in the streets.

Gerald Turner was born in 1931 with cerebral palsy. He lived in the mining village of Rawmarsh near Rotherham with his parents, three brothers and a sister.

There would be real fisticuffs, especially from my sister if ever someone started to make fun of me. My brothers and her stuck by me in our village when I were little. They used to take me out and play games so I could join in. Then if the other kids shouted names or nasty things about me my brothers would chase them and shout back. I couldn't walk then so sometimes it was difficult for them to get me very far in the old pushchairs because you didn't have proper wheelchairs then. In the evenings quite often one of my brothers would get me on his back and we would all go off to the cinema to see a picture. Then they could take turns in carrying me all the way there and back home.

Sometimes special toys would be made for a disabled member of the family, designed to help them overcome their disability. Before the last war most working class children had little or no money to spend on toys and they generally made them for themselves out of 'found objects'. Home made 'go karts' were extremely popular from the 1900s onwards and some were custom built by the children in the family for a disabled brother or sister.

Elsie Cooper had polio at the age of one in 1921 and remembers growing up as the youngest of a family of thirteen in Ponders End, North London.

I used to get very bored seeing my brothers run off and play. Sometimes they would push me out in my bath chair but of course it was difficult for them because I couldn't join in the same way. But I remember one summer that they decided to make a four-wheeler, a kind of trolley for me. They made it out of any old bits of wood from around the scrap heaps and soap boxes and some pram wheels one of them had found. That was great fun, being whizzed around on that. It made me more involved like in the fun of things, as children want to be. One day they even tipped me up in it near the river and I fell in! Arrived back home, all of us soaking wet.

Children with disabilities would often try to make their own aids or toys to suit their play needs and wants. Frequently the aim was to make themselves more mobile and at the same time to make their disability less obvious. For David Swift the ultimate aim was to hide his disability altogether and to make himself appear to be exactly the same as the other children.

> I used to go swimming in the canal a lot. I used to have my sister's bloomers and tighten them around me legs and in the water they used to blow up like a big balloon so you could float. I enjoyed going in the canal because while I was in the water nobody could see my legs. I always wanted to hide. I found a way of getting around better. I made a four-wheel trolley – we used to call them go-karts or soap boxes. We used to take all the palings out of the fences and get some old pram wheels. And this was ideal because it made me mobile and because I was sitting on it all I had to do was to steer it, didn't need to walk at all so no one could see my legs. I went everywhere on my trolley, even tried storing it in our front room so nobody'd pinch it. I could go anywhere then. I went all over the park, down in the woods. I used to keep it well oiled with cod liver oil. I loved it because I felt as if I sort of became invisible on it. I was just another kid, I was just somebody else.

Attempts to disguise a disability completely in this way were in most cases doomed to failure. The other children were usually extremely perceptive when it came to observing differences of appearance and behaviour. And a child who attempted to cover up his or her disability could be subjected to even more ridicule than they might otherwise have received. Consequently many children with disabilities often ended up rejecting the world that rejected them; they became outsiders and played alone.

David Swift only felt relaxed and free to express himself when he was playing where the other children could not see him.

> By being alone in the woods I could be myself, I could be free of watching eyes. I didn't have to perform as it were. I wasn't told off or called names there. Nobody spoke back to me. I used to pack a little bag of a few potatoes and a box of matches and I'd light myself a fire. And sometimes I would just sit there in the trees and think to myself. Then I would make up games for myself, get totally absorbed in them. I was everybody: Roy Rodgers, Hopalong Cassidy, Hiawatha. I used to strip off and run round the woods and put clay all over my body. It just seemed natural in the wood. I was just pretending and forgetting my life outside.

For children with disabilities who lived in the countryside there were often more opportunities to escape from the rigours of the children's culture. The street gangs that were such a dominant force on the city streets were less important in the villages. Also there was more physical space to escape into, with the countryside providing a great adventure playground in which children could – if they wished – be alone.

Disabled children were especially vulnerable in the rough and tumble world of children's play.

But some disabled country children chose, as their escape route, to work with adults on the farms and in the fields. There was always a big demand for child labour, especially at harvest time, and children who provided free labour were often warmly received even if they had a disability.

Ernest Williams was a partially sighted boy brought up in the village of Much Cowarne in Herefordshire in the 1920s. Although from infancy onwards he could see very little, he learnt much about farm life by making use of his other senses. As a result he proved to be of great value to his father, an agricultural labourer, and he spent much of his free time as a child in the fields.

I was left out of things simply because when it came to certain games it was obvious that I wasn't any good. For instance I could play tag all right. But I often tagged the wrong person, because people had clothes on that were similar, and you'd lose sight of one and catch up with another. And they'd check you off and say, 'It's not me you're tagging.' So I used to feel unhappy about being unable to be involved. And now and again it meant that you were the butt of a lot of ridicule. Kids are very cruel to each other. So consequently I didn't play very much with other children because essentially in the country, vision is vital. I know they used to look for birds' nests and this sort of thing in the seasons. Well, I couldn't see a bird's nest in amongst the hedges.

I used to help my father mainly. Out in the fields, well it was rather easier for me. I can't tell the difference between one cow and the next but my father used to direct me and I used to help him. I used to go out to the fields and help separate the milkers and so on. It was a funny thing but I really liked working with the animals. I could milk when I was about nine and I used to go down and milk quite often and if he wasn't around then I used to have a drink of the milk as well with my sister. I also used to have an interesting job in harvest time, I used to stand at the head of the lead horse so as to stop it moving when they were still loading. They used to call to me and I used to lead the horses forward for the next ten yards to a new area where the sheaves would be standing. I could tell where I was by smells. For instance, I could tell where I was if there were hops around. I could always tell when I was opposite somebody's door in the dark because of the smells of the wallflowers. And I could always tell which sack was which when I was helping with the feed because of the smells of the different grain.

I occasionally helped my father with a first time calver, a young heifer delivering her first calf. I remember being with him when one would get your hands into the back of the cow and ensure that the calf was correctly positioned and the head was down below the knees. And we would help her out with it. When she started to heave we would pull out the calf and it would slide onto the straw then the heifer would lick it. I was good at that because my hands were small and I liked the experience, kneeling in the straw and helping my father. And it was an enormous compensation to know that I could do that.

One of the few opportunities that children with disabilities had to meet and make friends with other disabled children was at the special clubs for them, which developed from the late nineteenth century onwards. There were clubs for deaf, blind and so called crippled children. However, many areas had no clubs at all and even where they existed the range of activities offered was often very narrow. Clubs like the Cripples Parlours were objects of derision amongst the able-bodied and children who went there sometimes faced further ridicule and abuse.

Betty Holland had polio in 1913 when she was nine months old. She lived in Camberwell, South-East London, the daughter of a printer.

There was nothing that I could do when I got home from school because I couldn't get out well enough to play in our street like the rest of them. I did used to go to the Cripples Parlour. It was a kind of club set up in an old church hall and it was every Monday. It was only for children with handicaps. It wasn't bad I suppose but you could only sit there, quite boring and play dominoes or cards, maybe have a chat. It was the name that got me. Cripples Parlour. As if that was the only place I was fit for and couldn't have had any fun anywhere else. I used to hate going

in there if people were looking because of them shouting out names to
you or laughing at you for going to a place with a name like that.

If boys and girls with disabilities were pushed towards the margins of their
own children's culture, there was much greater potential scope for integration
within the adult controlled education system. However, despite the rhetoric
of state education which increasingly claimed that it was providing for the
needs of disabled children, in fact schooling re-inforced the isolation of
children with disabilities. The children who were most isolated were those
who were not able or allowed to go to school at all.

In the 1920s the government estimated that there were around 20,000
'physically defective' children who were not attending school. Experts at the
time believed that the real number of such children was hidden from official
surveys and that it was closer to 50,000. For many local education authorities
were making no provision whatsoever for children with disabilities. The
poorest provision was in rural areas. Here the parents of a disabled child
might simply be told that their son or daughter would not be permitted to
attend school as their appearance and behaviour were likely to disturb the
other children.

Gerald Turner wanted to go to the village school with his brothers in
Rawmarsh.

I wasn't allowed to go to school with the rest because they said it
wouldn't be fair, that the other children might look at me. But I couldn't
understand that because I knew them all anyway. I saw them all and
played with them in the village. I used to get so frustrated and scream a
lot. I wanted to know what they were learning at school. When my
brothers came back from school at night I begged them to teach me the
things that they had been doing in the day. But they were too busy
playing out with their mates. They had no time. I just had to watch them
go off to school and wish it was me.

Much was left to the discretion of local education authorities and individual
headteachers. This led to much discrimination and many anomalies in the
treatment of disabled children. Some were permitted to attend primary school
but then found themselves prevented from receiving any secondary education
from the age of ten or eleven onwards.

Lorna Jacques was born in 1930 with cerebral palsy. She was the daughter
of a signalman and the family lived in Mansfield.

I went to the little school until I was ten. They used to wheel me down
there in a pushchair. But then all of us left to go to the big school. After
the summer holidays the headmaster at the secondary school said he
wouldn't have anything to do with me because I was disabled. I wouldn't
be allowed to go to his school and all the others were too far away. I

had to stay at home and listen to the radio. I was so disappointed that I wouldn't be able to learn any more at school, I thought it was the end of my life.

The parents of children who were denied schooling often did what they could to provide them with a basic education at home. Elsie Cooper:

I couldn't go to school until I was nine because there were no provisions at our local school for disabled children. So I stayed at home and my mother taught me to read. She did sums with me and I could write a bit and tell the time. We didn't have enough money to buy books and comics every week but we did have a couple of old books in the house. And if my father bought a newspaper she showed me on that. She showed me slowly all the letters, A-B-C and so on. Then I made up the words, then the sentences. She taught me to count with haricot beans.

Sometimes sympathetic teachers found a way around rigid school rules by giving disabled children private tuition out of school hours.
Ida Taylor, born in 1921 in Hertfordshire, had cerebral palsy.

They wouldn't let me go to school. They didn't want an invalid chair anywhere near the school. I always wanted to sit at a school desk though. I wanted to learn proper stuff like the others. When I was about eight, a teacher came to live next door to me and my mum. She knew that I wanted to go to school so she arranged that I could go to school with her for half an hour after all the other kids had gone home. I was made to sit up in a proper desk and to know what it was like. I learnt a bit of reading and stuff as well but then that teacher had to move so I had to stop going again. I never went into school after that. I used to get comic books from my mum and try to keep reading to myself but it was difficult.

The refusal of some local education authorities and individual schools to accept disabled children as pupils had little effect on those from a middle class background. Their parents often had the money to buy the education they wanted for their children. The most well-to-do and affluent would frequently employ a private governess who would come to the home to provide individual tuition for a disabled son or daughter. If the governess was good then learning could be an enjoyable experience for the child. But at the same time this kind of home-based education was often extremely isolating. Betty Leach:

First I had to go away to a private school which was in Bath. It was run by two ladies who were really very nice in a great lovely old house. It was a nice time but we did a lot of sewing. That's all we did very often which wasn't too good. A bit boring really and not much use to us later on. I was there for three years. After I got back home mother got me a special governess. She was a medical masseur and gymnast but she took all the school subjects too. I got on terrifically then. We never stopped learning. But she was so very expensive so when I was about fifteen she had to leave. After that it was a flop. There was absolutely nothing for me to do. I read the newspapers but I felt as though my proper learning was over.

Marjorie Hughes' father was a headmaster but her parents decided that it would be best for their daughter if she stayed at home and was educated there.

I did wish that I could go out to school. I went for three days when I was very young but I caught scarlet fever. After that my mother wouldn't let me go. She watched me so closely, because she thought I was more delicate I suppose. So I had a teacher at home for many years for about an hour every day. She was a dear soul and pressed on hard with the task of educating me. I had all the usual three Rs: reading, writing and arithmetic. But I was fond of history. I was so interested in all that. She encouraged me to read everything and also to listen to music. It was through her that a lot of my interests as a young person started.

Most middle class parents would send a disabled child to a small, local private school. There were thousands of such schools all over Britain, some of which sought to recruit disabled pupils. Private schools which catered for the disabled normally pitched their expectations very low and often made few demands on the children. This was particularly the case with girls' schools which provided a very narrow training for pupils.

Most children with disabilities however attended state schools. In the 1920s education officials estimated there were almost 100,000 disabled children at elementary schools run by local authorities. Again, many commentators at the time reckoned that the real figure of disabled children at school was double this. Most were simply not registered as such. The education they received varied greatly from one area to another and from one school to another. Generally the best provision for children with disabilities was in the big cities, especially London and Glasgow. Here there were even early attempts to provide free transport to school for children with special needs. In contrast in many villages and small towns lack of funds and a general lack of interest in this area meant that virtually nothing was done to provide for disabled children either inside or outside the classroom.

Children with disabilities seem to have been most effectively integrated into schools where headteachers encouraged the other children to show consideration towards their special needs.

Kenneth Matthews, born in 1923, had suffered polio when only months old. He started elementary school along with the other children in the Welsh town of Seven Sisters.

A disabled child pictured in a school classroom in the 1940s. Only a few schools made provision for the special educational needs of disabled children.

I was turned six when I went to school but I done very well at school. On my first day the headmaster called all the boys into the assembly hall. He explained to them all about me, what I'd got and what I'd been through. He sort of put them on their guard against banging me or bumping into me in the playground. I had to wear a black sling too so as they would all know which arm was the bad one. It was all skin and bones really because the muscles had been eaten away like. It was good that they all knew to take care of me. But I soon settled in and after a bit I made friends and got into scraps like all the other lads. I was a real good one-handed scrapper in the end.

Integration was also more likely when headteachers made an attempt to adapt the school curriculum so that disabled children could participate in as many activities as possible.

Louis Goldberg went to school in Brighton during the 1920s. He had cerebral palsy.

Our headmaster was an ex-professional footballer. I was the only disabled child in the school so on the first day he got me into his office. He wasn't nasty, he just said that just because I was disabled I wouldn't be let off anything. I was allowed to get into school a quarter of an hour before everyone and leave after they had all gone home because of the crowd and all the stone steps. Otherwise, I had to take part in all the school activities. That soon shook the shyness off me and I got on pretty well. If we were playing cricket I could join in a bit. If it was football I looked after all the boots and the kits and when the others were boxing I was made referee. They even tried to teach me to swim a bit. I used to enjoy it, being made a part of it all.

But in most schools there was no recognition that children with disabilities had special needs. Indeed there was often no recognition by teachers that they even had a disabled child in their class at all. With the large classes and rote teaching methods that were the norm before the last war, a child's disability could easily pass unnoticed. The learning difficulties that children experienced because of their disability were frequently misinterpreted by teachers as evidence of very low ability or even stupidity. As a result the children were often held up for ridicule and punished.

Ernest Williams was regarded as the school 'dunce' in Much Cowarne, Herefordshire in the 1920s.

From the outset it was pretty obvious that I wasn't following the normal pattern; I couldn't read in the ordinary way and of course I couldn't see the blackboard. But what actually happened was I was deemed to be not very quick on the uptake. So I rather got left out of it, I suspect. The teacher looked on me as not awfully bright and therefore not needing to bother with me. I used to sit at the back of the class because I wasn't so much in the focus of events then. And I could sit as obscure as I could be. But I didn't conform in the sense that I didn't pick up the glance from the teacher or a finger in my direction and so on. So I gave the answers when it wasn't my turn and eventually I'd get punished for that, because to the teacher it was disobedience. I had to stand in the corner sometimes as punishment. Usually I was put out of the way behind the teacher, the hope being that I wouldn't disrupt things. I remember standing in the corner or having to sit under the teacher's table out of the way. And I used to get sent down to the infants. I felt badly about that. I did feel as if I was having my nose rubbed into it.

Many children did not bring their disability to the attention of the teachers because they feared even greater persecution if their secret was revealed. They preferred their teacher to think they were stupid rather than to discover the truth. Marie Hagger:

I found it extremely difficult at school. Figures and numbers became a combination of jumble, mumbo jumbo. We had a big blackboard with an easel and the teacher would turn her back to the class to draw or write the numerals and the explanations that followed were all said with her back to the class so I couldn't try to lipread. When she turned round it was to say, 'Right, have you all got that?' Well, of course I hadn't even begun to get it. I couldn't hear and I wanted to cry my eyes out. So many times it happened that the rest of the lesson was just so much wasted effort because I wasn't grasping anything that she said. And every maths lesson I was into a fit of shaking all over before it started. Literally. Also I had this terrible feeling that she would find out sooner or later and I couldn't let that happen. Somehow or other, it didn't matter how much I tried to shrink myself, I came under scrutiny at various times. But very often the teacher would just dismiss me. Whatever I'd said, if it was wrong. She didn't know I was deaf after all, so she thought, 'Not so bright.' And do you know I'd rather preferred they thought I was not so bright rather than they guessed the truth. That was the fear part of my school life. Fear of being found out all the time, fear of being termed as different, fear of being held up for ridicule. And the more times I found myself in trouble the more I hated school as a whole.

Teachers also often made the assumption that children with disabilities were lazy. In fact they were often working desperately hard all day simply trying to hear or see the teacher's instructions. The immense difficulty and strain of this made some so tired they would occasionally fall asleep in class. Marie Hagger:

One day I remember the teacher was going to read us a play. All the children got excited about it. And she said she was going to take the different characters herself from the play and she wanted us to guess what the characters were. And she starts and I think after about five minutes I came over terribly tired. To be able to hear was – strain, strain, strain – the whole time. In fact, it's true to say I didn't know how to relax. So this particular occasion she started – drone, drone, drone – because that's how it came through to me, just a drone. I could hear the voice but what she was saying was another matter, the actual gist of the story was totally lost. I gradually felt myself going to sleep, dozed right off. Suddenly, bang on the desk. I was woken rudely. 'I've never come across such a lazy child in all my teaching history!' But I went along with that. Preferred her to think I was lazy or that I was not paying attention.

Very often on my school reports it would say, 'She's too lazy' or, 'She's very lazy' or, 'She could do better if she wasn't so lazy.'

One of the most common accusations of laziness against children with disabilities stemmed from a misunderstanding of the problems they experienced writing clearly. Genuine difficulties with holding pens and forming letters was seen as evidence of a careless and undisciplined attitude to work.

Margaret Bennett, born in 1925 with cerebral palsy went to school in Huddersfield.

The annual school photograph taken at Much Cowarne Village School in 1922. Ernest Williams was a pupil here until he reached the age of ten when a school inspector discovered that his eyesight was severely impaired.

I couldn't hold my pen properly at school. I always had a fear of the teachers coming and looking over my shoulder as I was writing my lessons because they would say what awful writing I had. 'That looks a nasty mess,' they used to say in front of all the class. You can imagine how that made me feel. It was absolutely awful. I held my pen in my own way and my mum even came to school and had a word with my form teacher to tell her that I couldn't do it any better. But it made no odds. The remarks went on as usual about what bad writing I had and why couldn't I do it like everyone else.

David Swift's disability led to a gradual loss of control over his hand movements while he was at school. The deterioration in his handwriting that resulted was severely punished.

I couldn't hold things in my hands properly and so my hand writing deteriorated, you know, it became scrawly, all over the page. And I remember the teacher saying, 'Swift, your handwriting is disgraceful!'

He got me out at the front of the class and he gave me the cane on my backside. And in them days you'd have no underpants on or anything like that, and very thin trousers. You were being punished twice but I just couldn't admit that there was something wrong with me because then the rest of the class would know, and once they found out, that was it.

Disabled children were also frequently punished for disobedience. But often what was deemed to be misbehaviour was an innocuous action that derived from their disability. This harsh treatment further heightened their feelings of fear and isolation. Marie Hagger:

Obviously when the teacher went out of the class, as soon as her back was turned, children would start talking. I could talk as well as the others but I never heard the teacher coming back in and the rest of the class stop chatting so of course I was always easily spotted for the one keeping on talking. The punishments increased, the length increased. They made me write lines out. It started with maybe fifty lines but it increased to seventy-five, one hundred, two hundred, even three hundred lines which I found very difficult. But I had to do it. 'I must not talk in class.' I didn't feel that I'd done anything wrong or that I'd committed a terrible sin or a crime. But that's how I was made to feel. Very often, standing outside the classrom door, there I'd be stood. The headmistress would be opposite to me and she'd see me. She'd look over her pince-nez spectacles that she wore then. 'You! I am surprised.' And I would feel about half an inch big. On other occasions it was standing behind the blackboard, which I dreaded.

Sometimes innocent actions were seen as provocative acts of defiance against the school authorities. They would be savagely punished, as David Swift remembers.

I used to be embarrassed if I was brought out in front of the whole class or in the assembly hall. I remember one morning I was in assembly and I was trying to snap my fingers. And suddenly I realised that I wasn't able to do this any more. The muscles in my hands had got worse. I stood there trying to flick my fingers. Couldn't snap my finger and thumb. The more I did it it seemed as though I was fidgeting. And one of the teachers come up behind me, grabbed me by the hair and dragged me across the floor and out of the hall. And I got the cane from the headmaster for doing that whilst assembly was on. I still didn't explain to him that my hands had gone because I was so embarrassed about my body.

In most state schools there was a great emphasis on the importance of sport and competitive team games. The belief that sport was 'character forming' was adopted from the public schools and achievement in sport became one of the most important sources of status in elementary school life. Children with disabilities would normally be expected to participate fully in school sports, though of course in many cases the teachers were not aware that the children in their charge had a disability. The children themselves were keenly aware of the importance of sport and some did their utmost to win. Often however their efforts ended in disappointment.

Marie Hagger remembers the annual sports days at her school in Tottenham in the 1930s.

Every year we had school sports day. It was quite an event. All the parents turned up. It was packed with people. And I entered for everything. I wanted to meet the challenge so I bunged my name down for practically every event, knowing I'd probably come last anyway. I would line up with all the others and the teacher would say, 'Ready, steady, go!' I didn't hear none of it. I'd wait for the others to run and then I'd run – and come last, of course. Same with skipping. I was a good skipper until I lined up against the others. Last again.

I was good at gymnastics and things like that but they weren't interested in those. It was the outdoor sports that really earned you merit. And at the end of the sports day the teacher would get the children to clap me even though I had come last in everything, just because I had taken part in all the races. I never felt so embarrassed.

Others did everything they could to avoid playing sports in order to avoid the ridicule that would follow from their inability to perform as well as the other children.

Ernest Williams as a partially sighted boy, found ball games very difficult.

I was never picked for the football team because I was no good at tracing the ball. But if there was nobody left and I had to be on one of the teams I was no good at ferreting the ball out but if it came my way I had a belt at it and that was it. And sometimes it went through the wrong goal and that wasn't any good to anyone, least of all me. So that occasioned a bit of ridicule. I couldn't play rounders either. I used to have a swipe at the ball with the bat and miss it and that always caused a lot of amusement. For that reason I didn't get involved if I didn't have to.

Olive Hall had contracted polio when she was twelve months old which left her unable to walk for many years. But at school she found that she was expected to do all the same sports as the other children with no consideration for her special needs. On one occasion this harsh and uncaring attitude almost lead to disastrous consequences.

I just had to get on with it at school. Nobody would let you off anything just because of how you was. Every Tuesday we were all taken swimming. The cubicles were all along the side of the baths I remember. Well, one particular day we had our swim, it was quite a long time to be in the water and some of the girls could swim very well. Of course I was weak because of the polio so I got tired easily when I did exercise. Then the teacher told us all to get out and change. She blew a whistle, I remember hearing that and I tried to get out of the deep end but then all my strength left me and I started to slide down, back into the water. All the water rushed inside me and I thought, this is it. But nobody noticed, none of the teachers even. After my friend Vera had got changed she went to tell the teacher I hadn't come to line up. Everybody thought that I must be larking on somewhere but then one of the girls spotted what looked like a dirty big rag on the bottom of the baths. It was me. One of the older girls jumped in and got me out. I was black and blue all over so they told me and the hospital told my mother I was lucky to be alive.

Some children with disabilities fantasised that they were great athletes and famous sportsmen. Their fantasies seem to have helped them cope with the pain of always losing and being rejected. David Swift:

At school you either joined in sports or you got five hundred lines. And basically I didn't want to be left out. Even when the whole school was doing cross-country I had to go as well and do exactly the same course as the rest of them. I ended up last of course, came into school about two hours after everyone else, red as a beetroot and dragging my legs on the floor. I went to the dining room to have my lunch but that was all gone and I'd come three hundredth in the race.

We were all mad keen on football at school too. I used to go and see Notts County play, specially Tommy Lawton. And I always wished that I could be like them, such fit looking men. Well when we played at school they used to pick two teams and nobody wanted me on their team. They used to stand arguing who was going to have me on their team. I would always be the one left over, feeling so embarrassed. If I did get a game then the lads would shout from the sidelines, 'You're meant to be injured after the game not before.' They would just bring attention to my legs all the time. So whilst they were making fun of me I used to dream about a comic character called Limp-Along-Lesley. He was in the *Hotspur* comic at that time. Limp-Along couldn't run at all on the pitch, his feet were so twisted up, but when he kicked the ball it would weave over the field and around all the players and steer clear of the goalie's hands. And I imagined that I was Limp-Along, he was someone that I could associate with, thinking about him really got me through those times.

One of the most traumatic school experiences of all for children with disabilities was being held up for ridicule. For some the most painful and difficult time in the school day was that spent in the playground. Ernest Williams was constantly derided by the other children for his misbehaviour in class, for his inability to play games and for his supposedly 'strange' appearance – he wore spectacles. The ridicule was most intense during playtimes at the village school. As a result Ernest frequently played truant, slipping out of the playground and spending the rest of the day in the fields.

I didn't get involved in the normal playtime things that the other boys got involved in because I couldn't identify with the things they did. A lot of things are conveyed by a glance in the appropriate direction. If they were looking at a certain bird, pointing at it, I got left out of these sorts of things because of my impaired vision. Fun-poking would result, unquestionably, from the fact that an incident would expose the fact that I couldn't see. I think I had the nick-name 'four eyes', 'cos I had glasses at one stage. Now that might well stir the other boys up to have a go at me. And I used to react to all this by simply cutting. At playtime I would nip through the railings and slip across the road in the shelter of the hedge and nip off home. The farmhouse where I lived was only a few hundred yards off and so I went back there and found things to do, perhaps feed the fowls or help my father in the fields. Nobody really noticed much on the farm. And in the afternoon my sister would come home with a note from the headmistress saying would my father please see to it that I was in school again next morning. But of course, I'd do it again if things got on top of me again.

David Swift remembers how during school plays his disability was cruelly exposed to all the children in the school.

All I needed was for someone to tell me I was doing well. But even thinking about the school plays, the parts they gave me were all highlighting my disability. Once I had the part of Long John Silver, the sea captain with one leg. The teacher had given me a real blunderbuss to put in my pocket. Then at the most important part in the play I had to draw the blunderbuss out and say, 'Back, back, you mutinous mob.'
   Well, on the night of the play when it came to the moment I couldn't get the blunderbuss out because my hands wouldn't work. And there was I, all the school watching me and I had to point two fingers instead and say, 'Bang!' It wasn't funny because then I knew that everyone would know about my hands. I didn't want them to know. I wanted to be like a chameleon, just fade into the background.

One of the most humiliating incidents at school for Marie Hagger occurred when she misheard an instruction from her teacher.

One day the teacher asked me to go to the hall to fetch something from a cupboard under the stage. I heard some of what she said but I missed a few words and I thought she had said, 'Bring some slippers from under the stage.' I found the box of slippers and duly presented them to my teacher. She rocked with laughter and said, 'Poor Marie has got it wrong. I don't think the parents can drink from these slippers!' She had actually wanted me to bring some cups and saucers that were in a big box. The entire class were laughing and I just wanted the ground to swallow me up.

There was little resistance to this harsh treatment of children with disabilities. The children themselves were usually too isolated and frightened to protest about any unfair treatment they felt they received. The only protests likely to happen were ones initiated by the parents, usually after a disabled son or daughter had been badly upset at school and had reported the incident at home.

Alice Maguire, born in 1909 in Croxton, Norfolk contracted polio when she was eight. Although she had severe difficulties in walking she recovered sufficiently to be able to attend the local school.

One day one of my friends picked me to do monitor duty with her in our class. But the teacher said to us, in front of all the other children, 'She's not being a monitor, I'd rather see a pin hopping around the room than see her.' She meant because of my bad legs and the way I walked. I went home very upset. Then that evening some of the other mothers and children came round to our house. They'd all heard what the teacher had said to me. Well, next morning, there was a riot at the school! My mum and some of the others went down and complained to the teacher. They shouted at her and really told her what they thought. And she left the school that morning. I don't know where she went. She disappeared for a week and when she came back she completely ignored me, never spoke to me again.

Some children passed through school without their disability ever being detected. However from the 1900s onwards more regular and thorough inspections of schoolchildren meant that increasing numbers of disabled children were detected by the authorities. The school inspector on his annual visit would sometimes discover that children regarded as backward were in fact trying to cope with a disability that the teachers had overlooked. In some cases the inspector would recommend that a disabled child be sent to an appropriate special school or institution. The visit of the school inspector to Much Cowarne school in 1925 dramatically changed Ernest Williams's life.

I would be sent into the infants quite often in school so that I was out of the teacher's way. On one particular occasion, the school inspector's visit was in prospect and they sent me into the infants as an elementary

precaution. When he came into the infants he spotted me there. I was
ten after all, while the other kids there were five of six. I recall that the
chairs were very small and I doubt if my bottom fitted properly into the
seats. I have a feeling that the teacher probably told the inspector, 'He's
a bit simple.' But the fellow, to his eternal credit, picked up a book and
said, 'Read to me, sonny.' And I opened the book and applied my nose
to the page as I always did and read to him. He just thanked me and
nothing happened just then but in a week my father had a note
commanding him to bring me to the Education Department in Hereford
and undoubtedly from that moment, I was destined to go into an
institution for the blind.

Medical inspections of schoolchildren were even more likely to lead to the
detection of children with disabilities in state schools. From 1907 onwards
the physical examination of children by the school authorities was made
compulsory. These examinations led to a growing awareness of the widespread
and serious nature of physical disability amongst working class children.

In 1913 the Chief Medical Officer to the Board of Education estimated that
of the six million children attending state schools in England and Wales large
numbers suffered from serious physical ailments. For example around ten per
cent were thought to have seriously impaired vision and around five per cent
had seriously impaired hearing.

However in many areas the education authorities had no wish to probe
too closely into physical disability amongst schoolchildren. Disability was a
potentially expensive problem to deal with and they did not want the burden
of extra expenditure. Thus school medical checks were not always as frequent
or as thorough as they might have been and even when cases of disability
were discovered, often little or no action was taken.

Marie Hagger remembers the day her deafness was discovered during the
first proper medical examination she received at school, at the age of ten in
1935.

One day at school I had a medical examination. It was a big event. Each
and every child at school was going to be medically examined to discover
whether there was anything amiss, to see how healthy we were or not.
This particular day all parents were asked to attend. My mother had no
option but to come. We girls had to strip to the waist with our coats
over our shoulders and sit in the hall and wait till our turn was called.
In I went. And I can remember this doctor's name to this day. And I
could describe her. She said 'Hello, come on in.' I stood right in front
of her. She went all over me, all over the body like they do. I turned
round and she pressed and pummelled and said to my mother, 'She's a
strong girl you've got here.' Turned me round again. 'Okay, turn back.'
She felt all my ears. I thought, well, when is she going turn me back
again. Eventually she did. She said, 'What did I say?' I felt my heart go

into my boots. I looked at her and said I didn't know. Here we go again, it sounds like blame on me. I'm in trouble. I saw it as trouble with a capital T. She said, 'Go stand in that corner with your face to the wall.' I did that and once again it was ages before I had to turn round. I thought, best not turn round until she says so. Then she clapped her hands. I turned round. 'Mother,' she said, 'did you know your child was deaf!'

My mother said she had just thought that I was backward. The doctor spoke to my mother in a low voice then she said to me, 'You're a fine girl but you're deaf.' I stood there absolutely frozen and the rest of that – I can't remember after that. It was just a blank. My mother carted me home. 'Well, what are you worried about? You knew'. I looked at her. For that moment I positively hated her. I was feeling ready to break. I thought my heart was broken. The pain, the anguish, the humiliation that I felt when I discovered that there was no going back on the fact that I was deaf. I went to my room and I think I cried for about three days. The tears just wouldn't stop.

The discovery of Marie's deafness failed to prompt any serious attempt by the school to cater for her special needs in the classroom. Like many other children she was sent to a clinic for treatment.

The day after my medical the headmistress sent for me. She put her hand on my shoulder and said, 'You're upset but don't worry, you must sit at the front of the class for all further lessons. And you are not going to a special school. It wouldn't be any use to you because you are too much on the emotional side where your hearing is concerned. I see no problems here provided you sit at the front.'

Well, I sat in the front of the class for one day. After that the teachers didn't even know what was wrong with me. They didn't know. I had the feeling that they either had not been told or they were pretending not to know. But it was back to the back of the class, nobody bothered. And carrying on with me not hearing.

But I had to attend a clinic twice a week so I missed an awful lot of lessons. They put tubes in my nose, both nostrils, and switched on a machine. It would, 'Br-r-r-r' – vibrate. Exactly what that's supposed to have done – anyone's guess. And I saw the doctor at the very beginning and he recommended this treatment. I never saw him again, not once. It didn't do very much because my deafness was more pronounced all the time. It was deteriorating and I knew it.

Medical examinations in state school were made compulsory from 1907 onwards. This led to a growing awareness of the widespread extent of physical disability amongst children in working class families.

The aim of clinic and hospital treatment was to try to improve the children's disability to a degree where they could participate in ordinary school life. This was seen as a cheaper and more effective alternative to actually providing for the special educational needs of disabled children in state schools. However the treatments and operations that the children received often failed. Sometimes it seemed to them that they were just being experimented upon.

This kind of experience could have a seriously disruptive influence on a child's schooling. Louis Goldberg's chance to take up a scholarship was lost through one such failed operation.

> I missed an awful lot of school because of hospital. I had to go up there three times a week for massage until I was ten. Then there were operations. The first lot of surgery wasn't too bad, they didn't really change that much. I got on quite well at school despite it all and eventually I was given a free scholarship to go to the technical college. But then when I was fifteen they mucked me up good and proper. I woke up after the operation and it hurt me even to breathe too hard. The Cantor was there chanting the psalms, giving me the last rites. All the ligaments in my left hip had been cut and my hip had been cut away at. I had just been experimented on and I was never the same again. I couldn't take up my scholarship, I had to try to learn to walk all over again.

Constant visits to clinics and hospitals also increased the sense of isolation and aloneness of children with disabilities. David Swift was sent into hospital to try to discover the cause of his disability.

> I was so alone as a child. In hospital I remember I was having a lumbar puncture to see what was wrong with me, to see if it was polio. And if you've ever had a lumbar puncture, you don't want a second, which I did have. And I coped with it all on my own as a twelve year old child. It was so painful. But nobody came to see me. And at twelve then you went into a ward for men, I was so alone. Even now I can remember the smell of the place, having to cope with it. Then I had to go to the clinic on my own every week. It didn't help. They couldn't even tell what was wrong with me.

Some of the children who were discovered to have some physical impairment would be sent to a special school. A whole range of local authority run special schools grew rapidly from the turn of the century onwards to cater for sick or disabled children.

The fastest expansion was in open air schools for pupils with rickets, bronchial complaints and physical problems resulting from malnutrition. The first British open air school was opened in 1907 by the London County Council at Bostall Woods, Woolwich. Others followed all over Britain so that by the eve of the Second World War there were more than

An open-air class in the North-West in the 1930s. By 1939 there were more than 150 open-air schools all over Britain catering for almost 20,000 children with physical impairmants.

one hundred and fifty open air schools providing for almost 20,000 children.

This was the kind of special provision that local education authorities were keen on for it was very cheap. All they had to do was to rent a small plot and erect temporary wooden classrooms and accommodation. The children were usually sent away for a period of three to four weeks. Some children went as day pupils for longer periods of several months. The schools subjected children to a spartan regime which included lessons in the open air, compulsory eating of 'healthy' foods and a rest period in the middle of each day. Their organisation reflected the great inter-war belief in the invigorating and curative powers of fresh air, sunshine, sleep and exercise.

Often the schools did promote minor improvements in the health of poor working class children who were normally deprived of food and who lived in overcrowded homes where disease was rife. However the social and psychological effect of the schools on the children sent there was often less positive. 'Open air' children were derided by their able-bodied peers as weak and sick, and the harsh treatment of the children who went to these special schools did nothing to improve their confidence or self-esteem. The discipline in these places was often even more strict than in the elementary schools.

Reg Chamberlain was one of the 4,000 children sent from London elementary schools every year during the 1930s for a few weeks at an open air school. He was sent from his home in Clapham to spend some weeks at the Royal Canadian Open Air School in 1927 because he was suffering from rickets.

There were so many of us in our street who were ill simply because of the conditions then. There wasn't enough food to go round our family and quite regular I would go to bed hungry. I was very small as a child and when I was about ten they found out I had got rickets and as a result my legs were thin and misshapen. The school decided to send me off to an open air school for a few weeks. It was in Bushey in Hertfordshire. A lovely big country place but with huts and a sort of square, with all open sides that us boys had to sleep in. The master used to walk around with a big cane, and we used to call it 'The Bushey Bender'.

They were very strict. All our thoughts were to escaping, how we could get out and get back home. I was dying to leave and go back home but you had to have put on some weight in order that they would let you home. I was so nervous on the last morning when I was going to be weighed. And luckily for me I had put on one pound so they let me go.

Most of the special schools for disabled children were day schools. From the 1890s onwards it had been the statutory duty of local authorities to

Blind children pictured reading braille in a day school in the 1930s. It had been the statutory duty of local authorities from the 1890s onwards to provide special education where necessary for blind and deaf children.

Children leaving to go home at the end of the day at Peterborough Special School, London in 1906. Many of the pupils were embarrassed to attend such a school, reinforcing their image of themselves as abnormal children and outsiders.

provide special education where necessary for blind and deaf children. Many did nothing and justified their inaction on the basis they had very few deaf or blind children in their schools. Some even claimed that no children with these disabilities were born in their area. However those that did take their duties seriously – usually big cities like London, Liverpool and Glasgow – quickly developed day schools for children suffering from ophthalmia, myopia, partial vision and deafness.

When Phyllis Jones was born in 1926 she was partially sighted. Although she lived with her parents she was able to attend a myopic day school just outside her home town of Sheffield in the 1930s.

We went to school every day on a bus 'cause it was right far out in the country. It was on a big field and we could go out playing a lot, better than if we'd been in the town like the other schools were. I didn't mind going at all 'cause you got to know a lot of friends and we all had bad sight and so the teachers had to help us with the writing, big letters and that. They weren't real strict with us. I remember my maths teacher used to spend a long time trying to get me to do sums and to write all the times tables out because I couldn't read the numbers in the proper books. It was a bit strange sometimes when we went home after school. My brothers and sisters all went to school in town and so did their friends and my friends from school lived all over. I usually could only see them at school. But anyway my mother used to make sure that my sisters took me out with them to play and the other kids in our street used to look after me as well 'cause they knew I went to the myopic school and I couldn't see as well as them. It was just like having two separate lots of friends.

Local authorities also provided a number of day schools for 'crippled' or 'physically defective' children. They often had very low expectations of what the children might achieve and most of the school day would be spent performing simple manual tasks. Betty Holland was sent to a Cripples' School near her home in South-East London during the 1920s.

I went to a school for handicapped children. I could read a bit when I went there but we just had baby lessons at that school. Very basic things like the A-B-C and adding up two numbers. They treated you like imbeciles. Dressmaking was the main subject, well, needlework. It was all we learnt. We used to sit for hours stitching. I never knew what good it was going to do me in life, to get a job and that. I hated it and so I was no good at all at sewing. First you had to learn how to do a buttonhole. You had to sit there and do those until you were perfect then you could move onto making a garment of some sort. Well, I never got past the buttonhole at all. I was on buttonholes for years.

The level of provision and status of these 'cripple' schools was so low that they did little to change the prejudices against children with disabilities. Many of the pupils were very embarrassed that they had to attend such a school, reinforcing their image of themselves as abnormal children and outsiders.

Minnie Parsons was born in Birmingham in 1929. When she was three she was run over by a horse drawn coal cart. The accident left her leg so badly fractured that it never mended. She was sent to the Cripples' Day School in Green Lane, Borsley Wood.

After the lessons all us kids had to lie outside the classroom in the playground in the afternoon for our rest. We were all disabled, different

A lesson at Peterborough Special School in London in 1906. The authorities often had low expectations of what disabled children might achieve and so most of the day would be spent in very simple lessons or doing basic manual crafts.

kinds of things wrong with us. Well, the playground was a short cut for people to get through to the shops and they used to stand and stare at us kids lying out on their way. Well this would make you feel upset, wouldn't it? Sometimes it used to get me down. I used to feel ashamed and embarrassed. So I used to try and go back home in the break times to my mum. Our house was only up the road, along the school railings and on the corner. But my mum always took me back, there was no getting out of it.

CHAPTER THREE

ANOTHER WORLD

In 1923 nine years old Ted Williams became an inmate of The Royal Manchester Road School for the Blind in Sheffield. He lost his sight a year before after a pop-gun accident outside his home. But he was an independent, streetwise boy, one of a family of fifteen, used to roaming free in the city slums. To him the institution where he was forced to spend the rest of his childhood seemed worse than prison. Even its architecture and design – a Victorian gothic monolith, then totally unsuited to the needs of blind children – he found intolerably oppressive.

> I was playing around with a boy in the playroom and I banged my eye on the corner of a cupboard. Now this cupboard was put in a ridiculous place because any blind child playing around would bang their head on it. I'll tell you what I did. I know I shouldn't have done but still. I systematically kicked it in, I broke it into splinters.
>
> And on another occasion I cut my head quite badly on a window in the greenhouse. The greenhouse was put in the most stupid position where we used to run around outside the school building. What I did, I took my shoe off and broke every single window in that greenhouse. One by one, I smashed every pane of glass. You can well imagine the punishment I got for doing things like that. I got the stick, I got the cane, I got lectures, I was made to apologise at least a thousand times, I was put into Coventry, I was told how wicked I was to break school property. I had the name of rebel. But I just had to do it. My resentment against the place just came to the surface and boiled over.

Ted Williams was one of around 50,000 children with physical disabilities who had to endure a harsh institutional upbringing at this time. There were a variety of different institutions, all of them rigidly sex segregated. Some were geared to dealing with a particular disability. In the 1920s for example there were more than five hundred institutions catering for children with physical disabilities including seventy-seven for the blind, fifty for the deaf and seventy-eight for so called 'physical defectives'.

However, many children with a variety of physical disabilities ranging from cerebral palsy to epilepsy were lumped together in Dickensian workhouse wards and orphanages. Others languished in asylums and mental hospitals all over Britain. This was the heyday of the live-in institution and there was a wide acceptance that it was right to segregate these children from the rest of society. Their appearance and behaviour was often seen as disturbing or offensive and it was thought best to remove as many of these children as

A geography lesson at Elm Court Blind School in West Norwood in 1908. There was a widespread acceptance at that time that it was right to segregate these children from the rest of society.

possible into institutions. As a result of entrenched opinions like these, between the 1900s and the 1950s more than a quarter of a million disabled children would grow up in these places.

Many of these institutions were run and controlled by private charities. The needs of physically disabled children had always been a low priority for the government and provision in this area was traditionally dominated by voluntary societies with little monitoring by government inspectors. Little money was made available to these institutions. Consequently they were often severely overcrowded, chronically short of funds and run by lowly paid and untrained staff.

The vast majority of the children who entered institutions for the physically disabled were from working class homes. Many came from the poorest families in the slums, for much physical impairment was a consequence of severe deprivation and hardship. This close association between poverty and disability in the minds of charities and government officials helped to fuel extremely hostile attitudes towards the children. Many of the prejudices made about the undeserving poor by middle class reformers were heaped upon them. They were part of the 'great unwashed' who were ignorant, immoral and feeble-minded. In short they needed to be saved from themselves and from their families. One of the main aims was to instill into them a discipline which would prevent them from begging, living on poor law handouts and becoming a public nuisance.

Many believed that these institutions were involved in a high minded and Christian activity of child saving. Their constant fund raising appeals and annual reports were often sentimental or even idealistic in their aspiration for a better life for the children in their care. But the well scrubbed, smiling faces on the front covers of magazines like *Brothers and Sisters* produced by The Children's Union masked what was really happening in these institutions. In fact their underlying purpose was to crush the individual personalities of the children that arrived and shape them into a narrow and rigidly conformist mould. They were to be trained to perform simple tasks and to do as they were told. This process began the very first day the children arrived. Like prisoners, the newcomers were deloused, their hair was shaved, their clothes were taken from them and they were issued with the institution's uniform. They were also given a number. This was their new institutional identity. For the children it all came as a terrible shock.

In 1935 twelve year old Mary Baker was sent to The Halliwick Home for Crippled Girls, a Church of England institution for physically and mentally disabled girls. She had a dislocated hip as a result of which she walked with a limp. Mary was the daughter of a Dorset agricultural labourer who was wounded during the First World War, and she had three brothers. When her mother died in 1933 the authorities decided that her father would be unable to bring up the children and they were sent to the workhouse at Wimborne Minster. From there she was separated from her brothers and dispatched to Halliwick.

When I first arrived at Halliwick the nurse took me into this bathroom and she stripped me off completely. She cut my hair short, right above the ears. And then I was deloused with powder of some description. Then they put me in a bath and scrubbed me down with carbolic soap. It was very degrading to me. And I felt as though the end of the world had come and so I cried, I sat in the bath and cried my eyes out. At any rate they told me it was no good in crying and dried me down. They used such rough towels it felt like they were sandpapering me. Then I was dressed in the Halliwick uniform, navy blue socks, stockings and a gym slip and a serge jumper and I was taken up into the dormitory, a big huge room it seemed, with about ten beds in it. I went in there and lay down on my new bed. I felt awful and I thought that nobody cared for me. Anyway, I don't think that I slept that night, I felt so lonely. I didn't know what to do, had no idea what I was going to do. But it was huge and it was lonely, the place. And I felt really lost and I thought, What am I going to do with no one to love me?

I had entered a different life. My father was far back home and I thought that everyone had forsaken me. I think I cried most of the night. So this was my start. The next morning you were given a number and

Brothers & Sisters

THE MONTHLY MAGAZINE OF

THE CHILDREN'S UNION.

Patron: H.R.H. The Duchess of Gloucester.

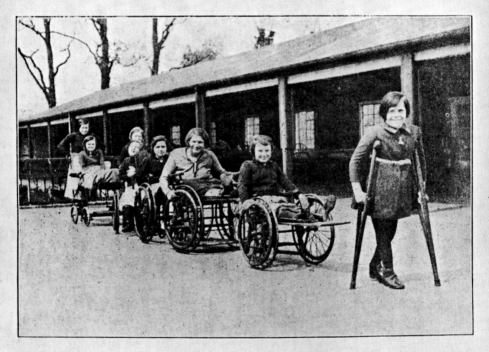

HERE WE ARE, TO WISH YOU A VERY HAPPY NEW YEAR
FROM ALL AT ST. NICHOLAS' HOSPITAL, PYRFORD.

No. 538   PRICE 1d.   JANUARY, 1938

*The well-scrubbed smiling faces on the front covers of magazines like this one
from* Brothers and Sisters, *produced by the Children's Union masked the
harshness of many institutions for disabled children.*

A class of girls at The Halliwick Home for Crippled Girls in the 1930s. Mary Baker was sent to Halliwick in 1935 when she was twelve years old.

you had to remember it. My number was twenty-nine and when I got up and went to wash, my towel and flannel had my number on them. Twenty-nine was engraved on all my hairbrushes and things with a big hot poker like thing. Everything I owned had a marking of twenty-nine on, so I can never forget that number. Our lockers in the playroom had the same number and our clothes were marked with our numbers, so we knew what we had. We were hardly ever called by our first names, only by the other girls. And if matron wanted you she called you by twenty-nine or whatever number you had. We never had names, we were just numbers there. It was all very disciplined. I couldn't make it out at first, why we should all have numbers and not names. I felt a bit low about it. I couldn't really put my feelings into an expression, only that I felt very lonely about it.

Nine year old Ted Williams's arrival at Manchester Road School for the Blind in Sheffield in 1923 was similarly traumatic.

The first day you got there, you changed into the school uniform and your own clothes were put in the wardroom. And to add insult to injury, we were each dumped with a number. Mine was forty-three, prisoner

Forty-three sort of thing, and I kept that number for seven solid years. Well I accepted that I was Forty-three, I didn't really kick up rough against that because it was part of the system. And it got to be part of your life. I was told that every child had a number, 'And your number, Williams, is forty-three,' 'Williams', they used to say, enough to say, 'You serpent', you know. 'Your number is forty-three and you will keep that number until we decide different'. No question that I didn't want a number. All my clothing, all my possessions, what few I had anyway, I discovered there was a big number forty-three. We had to line up for everything in our convict numbered sequence. And you must not get at the back of the wrong number. Me being forty-three, if I got at the back of fifty-three I got punished. I believe that's what they used to do at Wormwood Scrubs. The result was that I felt very homesick. It seemed to be a tremendous size – that was the thing that impressed me at first, it seemed a big parochial place to me.

I remember the first night, what a night. I just laid you see and thought about home and wished I was back. I just cowered down under the sheets, beautifully clean, but wickedly cold and I just cowered down underneath pulling the bedclothes over my head, just had a little cry until I got some of it out of me. My home wasn't much to crack about. We lived in what was then the slum area of Sheffield and me mother and father had all us kids to feed and clothe. We didn't have much and what money we did have, well, me mother was a bit careless. She had developed what could really have been a good business, reading the cards, telling fortunes, but I don't know, the money just disappeared. Sometimes she'd put her hand in her pocket and get hold of a handful of silver from her card reading and throw it down on the floor for us kids to play with to keep us quiet. And every Thursday, with me being blind, she used to take pity on me, you see, and they'd give us extra bacon bits or something like that. I was used like that.

Mind, she had to do that because we never had enough to eat in our house. For instance, me mother used to have to pawn any decent clothes we had on Monday night and on a Friday she'd get them out of pawn, if she had enough pennies to do it. And that was just so as we could eat all week.

But I remember when the dictate came from the council saying that I had to go away to Manchester Road School, I didn't want to go. You see, it doesn't matter how bad your home is, you still feel homesick when you leave it, home's still the thing.

The initiation of new children into the institutional regime was not always as harsh and brutal as this. For example in the RNIB Sunshine Homes for blind children and in some of the more liberal and progressive deaf schools there was a more gentle approach which attempted to make the children feel at home. Nevertheless, because these institutions took children away from their families at a very young age the first few weeks were often a very distressing time for the new infant inmates.

In 1932, five year old Hazel Boucher had to leave her family in Brigg, near Scunthorpe, to begin her first year living in at the Yorkshire Residential Institution for the Deaf in Doncaster.

> When I first came to the baby school, when I was five, I came with my mother. We had a look around the school then suddenly my mother had gone – I didn't realise at first and then I started looking for her and couldn't find her, she'd disappeared and I started crying. I remember having a dummy in my mouth and I was crying and crying and missing my mother. And then for a few days I had to settle down and live with the other children and start to play with the toys there. On the next Saturday when my mother came to visit me I started to remember, oh that was my mother, it seemed a long time since I had seen her. She took me round the shops in Doncaster for the afternoon. And then I realised that I was coming back to school so I clung to a lamp post saying, 'No, no, I don't want to go back to school. I want to go home with you.' My mum was dragging me. She says, 'Come on, come on you've got to go back into school.' And anyway she brought me in, then she went off home and I was left there on my own again.

Many institutions tightly regulated and restricted contact between the children and their parents. Once they were left at the institution many didn't see their parents for months or even years. Visits often had to be arranged by appointment through the principal of the institution. Applications by mothers and fathers would be refused if the meeting was considered inconvenient or inappropriate by the institutional authorities. The aim was to reduce the opportunity for what was seen as the corruption or contamination of the child by its family. If the child came from a very poor working class background the parents were invariably viewed as a bad influence, contact with whom should be kept to a bare minimum. This was one important way in which the institution aimed to exert absolute control over its inmates. They were extremely successful in this respect. Most parents found it too difficult to visit their children on a regular basis. Even more simply did not have the money or the means to get there as many children lived in institutions far away from the parents' home. And in some cases one or both the parents were dead. Visits were a very rare occasion in the institutional routine.

Marjorie Jacques, born in Guildford in 1920, contracted polio when she was eleven months and as a result was unable to walk. She was sent to Chailey Heritage Craft Institution near Lewes in Sussex from the age of three to ten.

> We only had one visiting day a year all the time I was at Chailey. I used to miss my parents so much, I used to cry myself to sleep. The homesickness was really terrible and we were only allowed home in the

One of the RNIB Sunshine Homes for blind children set up after the First World War which adopted a more liberal and sensitive approach to residential schooling for blind children.

Christmas and summer holidays which were marvellous. I remember that if I was naughty at home my mum used to say she would send me back to Chailey early. I would do anything rather than go back early, that was really like holding a gun to my head. The night before I had to go back, I used to cry myself to sleep. As soon as we arrived back at Chailey they took our own clothes away and parcelled them up and out came the dreaded uniforms.

Even where more regular visiting was allowed, for example in hospital institutions, there were often elaborate rules restricting contact between children and their families. Some specified that no brothers or sisters should be permitted entry. Others barred direct contact with parents and only allowed visiting mothers to look at their children through windows.

In 1928 five year old Jeanne Hollamby left her home in Beckenham, South London to go to Tite Street Children's Hospital, Chelsea to be treated for cerebral palsy. She was to remain there for five years.

I was in hospital for five years and my mum used to visit me every week but she wasn't allowed into the ward, not once in all that time. She just looked in through the window in the ward door and waved at me like all the other parents. That was really upsetting, much more upsetting than if we'd have had proper visits. She used to leave me presents to have when she had gone home but of course it wasn't like seeing her properly. All year we looked forward to the garden fête in the summer so then we could be with our mums properly for an hour or so.

The children often tried to keep in touch with their family through letters home but most institutions operated an extraordinary system of censorship which prevented the young inmates from telling their parents the truth about what was happening to them. Mary Baker:

When we were in the classroom we used to write home every week. After we had all written a letter the headmistress passed them all on to the matron so she could read them. And she used to cross off what we weren't supposed to put in. We had to put that we loved it there, and everybody was happy, and everything that was really lies. We couldn't put any of our true feelings into a letter. If we had written anything bad about the place they were brought back to us and we had to write them out again, leaving out those bad things. Then they were passed back to the matron and sealed down and sent off. I used to write to my father and to my grandmother. And I used to get letters back saying they were so thrilled that I was so happy. But my letters were all lies.

Separated from their family and suddenly finding themselves alone in a strange institution where most of the adults seemed to be harsh and unsympathetic, many children experienced deep loneliness and fear. They coped by turning to each other for support and friendship.

Ted Williams remembers how he made the most important friendship in his life on his very first day at Manchester Road School for the Blind in Sheffield.

I was sent into the washroom to wash my hands before the tea and as I was standing there the boy next to me asked me who I was. And I said, 'Williams' in a sort of fading voice, because by that time I was all but crying. And he introduced himself. He said he was Charlie and that he was seven and he'd been at school since he was five so he knew the ropes like. After he'd washed his hands, he said he would have to go now, because you couldn't hang around once you'd finished or the teachers would oust you. But as he was leaving Charlie said, 'I'll see you in the square.' I had no idea where that was but after a bit someone showed me and it was a playground for us boys. But when I got in there I was at an absolute dead loss. And I stood with me couple of fingers in me mouth, just wondering what to do. And one or two of the blind children half bumped into me and said, 'Who's this?' And I said, 'It's me', so they said, 'Who's me?' And I told them, 'Williams.' After a while some big fourteen or fifteen year old lad accidentally walked into me and said 'Who's this?' And I said, 'Williams'. And he says, 'Oh, are you one of the new kids?' I said, 'Yes' and well he said, 'What thou stood there for? Are you looking for anyone?' and so I said, that I was looking for Charlie. He says, 'Well, why don't thou shout him? Shout him at the top of your voice – we shout people here when we want them.' So I just stood there shouting 'Charlie' and eventually he heard me and followed me voice and found me. Now that was the start of a life long friendship.

Mary Baker remembers the strong camaraderie that developed amongst the girls at Halliwick in the 1930s.

The most places where we felt lonely was in our bedrooms, in the dormitories, because we all used to chat about the things we'd lost, our mothers, our fathers and our brothers and sisters. We all used to cry and we wondered when we would see them again. At any rate, at times like that I used to read stories to the other girls in the room because some of them didn't know how to read. But we had to be careful not to get caught, it was all so disciplined. There was no love at all. But we used to read together and talk and get by that way. I think I cried with most of them girls and so we made different friends. And I think sometimes the friendship was more than we should have had, because we used to cuddle in to one another and accept that as what we needed, what we couldn't get at Halliwick so we got it that way.

Of course, sometimes we had high jinks as well, we used to have pillow fights and all the things that girls do. We made our own fun that way.

Institutional life in the 1930s. Separated from their family and finding themselves alone in a strange institution where most adults seemed to be unsympathetic many children experienced deep loneliness and fear.

But we were frightened to do too much in case someone came and you'd get into trouble. And if matron did catch any of us we all stuck up for one another. If anyone got into trouble, we'd accept the responsibility instead of them, we'd never shy on a person.

Friendships were also very important in helping deaf children cope with institutional life. The insistence that children use lip reading and the oral method often heightened their feelings of loneliness and isolation. Sign language was normally banned in the classroom and at mealtimes, but children would sign to each other in their free time, usually in the playground. Signing enabled them to communicate more easily and naturally, encouraging close friendships. Because signing was taboo in most institutions children from deaf families who could already sign would often teach children from hearing families how to sign in the playground. Dennis Boucher was sent to The Yorkshire Institution for the Deaf at the age of seven in 1933.

When I first came to school not many of the children could sign. They just used 'F' for father and 'M' for mother. They didn't know the alphabet at all; They didn't know any signing. I could sign because my older brothers came home and taught me when they went to the Leeds school.

Language instruction in a deaf school in the 1940s. During the first half of the century most British deaf schools adopted the oral method and signing was banned.

And so when I saw a rat running across I did my sign for rat and the other children said, 'R-A-T for rat.' And they said, 'Rat, is that how you spell it?' And it went on and on and on and gradually it spread around and they all learnt how to spell rat in sign.

And I carried on teaching signs like mother, father, brother, sister – I taught them all those. And they all found it very interesting and they enjoyed it. And they all gradually picked it up. It spread round the whole of the little school. We weren't allowed to sign in the classroom but in the playground they would sit around me and I would show them different signs. All the different animals and pigs and cows. I was explaining to them and they're all saying, 'Is that a cow, is that a horse, is that a pig?' So soon they could all sign and we used to sign together in the playground and that was good.

In most of the institutions practically every day in the year seemed the same to the child inmates. The institutional day was organised into a series of closely supervised routines. From half past six in the morning until eight at night there would normally be a compulsory and standard sequence of tasks like washing, mealtimes, school lessons, work, and so on, the changeover between which would often be punctuated by the blowing of whistles or the ringing of bells. Apart from at playtime silence between the inmates would be enforced for practically the whole day. The children enjoyed no rights, no privacy and very little free time. They were forced into compliance with this regimented routine by the use of harsh discipline and punishments. The design of this kind of authoritarian regime was partly administrative convenience for understaffed and overcrowded institutions. But there was a more fundamental aim, to eliminate any independent thought or action of the children. Such a regime made it possible – at least in theory – for institutions to exert total control over the thoughts and feelings of the children in their charge, thus enabling them to shape their minds and their bodies in whatever way they thought fit. The routine at Manchester Road School for the Blind in Sheffield in the 1920s – still vividly remembered by Ted Williams – was typical of this kind of regime.

The rules about silence in the school were terrific, they were out of this world. Say a meal time, five minutes before a meal time, the teacher would come up to the playroom and blow a whistle, that meant all the boys were to line up. Then we marched in absolute dead silence from the playroom – we didn't walk, relaxed walk – it was a semi goose-stepping march. They called it being smart and upright. And we mustn't slouch along and we mustn't speak. If you accidentally walked a bit fast and bumped into the boy in front of you and you giggled or passed some comment, my word that was fifty lines 'I must not talk in line'. And that applied for the whole meal. Any talking and they would ask, 'Who's that talking?' Of course, we tried to avoid being caught but they always

A lesson for children in a mental handicap hospital in the 1940s. In most institutions every day was a series of closely supervised and organised routines.

found out and they would shout out the punishment, fifty lines or staying in at playtime, whatever it was. You must never speak without permission.

Bryan Dive, born in 1932 with cerebral palsy, remembers a similar insistence on silence at Henwick School for Cripples in Northampton where he spent much of his childhood.

We weren't ever allowed to speak in the dorm. If you were caught talking then your whole dorm would have to go to bed early without any dinner perhaps for a few days or a week. That was an awful punishment because it caused trouble for you with the rest of your mates. The teachers knew that so it was one of their favourite punishments of us. Well once I was caught talking when I shouldn't have been and the teacher made my whole dorm suffer by going to bed early for a week. Some of the boys got angry with me and they got violent in the dorm. And some of them hit me because I had got us all into trouble.

The dining room at Elm Court Blind School in West Norwood in 1908. Discipline was strictly enforced at mealtimes when the children were expected to eat what was put in front of them in absolute silence.

Discipline was equally strictly enforced at mealtimes when the children were expected to eat whatever was put in front of them. There was never any choice at all and uneaten food refused by individual children would be served up for them again for the next meal. The main problem however was the lack of food. Marjorie Jacques remembers mealtimes at Chailey Heritage School in the late 1920s.

The food was really dreadful. Regularly every morning, burnt, lumpy porridge for breakfast and brown bread with lardy margarine. Dinner-time I can only ever remember stews, I don't think we ever had anything different. And potatoes, they made you eat them boiled in their skins with all the eyes still in. And they would walk around the dining room whilst we were all eating to make sure that you didn't leave anything. You'd eat it all or you'd have it dished up for tea, or even breakfast the next day. Tea time was brown bread, marg and a dollop of treacle on the side of your plate. Sometimes it would be that horrible black cooking treacle. We never got any real treats at all. I know that sometimes we actually used to eat sweet grasses in the field where we played because we were that hungry.

Central to the regimented institutional routine was the idea that the children should remain within the building or the grounds at all times. Many institutions were circled by high walls and railings or were located in remote rural locations – often run as self sufficient 'colonies' – to ensure that contact with the outside world was minimised. There were few opportunities to go outside the institution apart from the occasional holiday at home if this was possible or permitted. Ted Williams remembers the one occasion when he was allowed out without supervision.

One day I was called into the office and as I went in the schoolmaster said 'You've got a visitor' and it was my father, well, that was something out of the ordinary all together and he said, 'I've got permission for you to come home, your mam's died'. I was about thirteen and a half at the time. So Mr Maddox said I could go home for the funeral. And I was taken home there and then. I went in school uniform but when we got home me father gave me some borrowed clothing. And we had this funeral, I think she got buried at 2 o'clock. And we adjourned, supposedly for like they have, a funeral tea. But I was under strict orders to be back at school for half past four. My father had to tell them when the funeral was and everything and so I was back here for half past four and that was that. I was left pretty much to meself, nobody sat and talked to me about what had happened at all. I spent several days crying to meself and thinking a lot in bed. It impressed me so much that I made up a poem. There were five verses to the poem and it started . . .

> 'Oh death, thou cruel death who takest all away,
> Why dost thou deal so cruelly, nor does falter nor delay.'

For some children the only time they left their institution was to go to a hospital for treatment. But the standard of medical care given to institutional children was usually low. Some who endured successive operations to cure their disability felt they were being experimented on.

Bill Elvy was born in 1918 in Sittingbourne, Kent, the son of a stockman. He had severely deformed hands and feet which prevented him from walking. When he was still only a young child the authorities decided that it would be best for Bill to live in an institution for crippled children. From there he would be sent out to hospital for the various operations that they had planned for him.

They operated on me when I was still very young. It was so frightening. In and out of hospital all the time I was. You couldn't have any visitors and anyway my parents couldn't afford to come 'cos the hospital was in London. I used to have to live in the Shaftesbury Home to get ready for them doing operations on me. But you got no real care there even though they must have known how bad the operations were and how much pain I was in. They were meant to prepare me, build me strength up kind of thing for carting me off for the next operation on me hands or me feet. But it was very harsh. You more than likely got a clout round the ear or a wallop rather than caring. It was like prison to us kids. All our letters were censored, in and out. You were there to do your chores, hard graft and try and keep your head down as far as I could see. Then the hospital would ring and say, 'Right, let's have him in for another op.' And off I'd be sent for some more torture at the hospital.

The fear engendered by surgery and medical experimentation was greatest in long stay hospital wards. Thousands of disabled boys and girls spent long periods of their childhood as hospital patients. Here the enforcement of strict institutional discipline and a mistaken belief in the complete immobilisation of some patients meant that occasionally children were not allowed to move at all in or from their beds.

Susan Miller contracted polio in 1921 when she was just a year old. She was sent straight into hospital from her home in Chiswick, West London. Susan was to remain in hospitals until she was twenty-one years old.

From the age of five until I was thirteen I was encased in a plaster cast, rather like an Egyptian mummy in the children's ward of the Royal Sea Bathing Hospital in Margate. Whenever the little girl in the next bed to me wanted to play 'dollies' I undid the straps that were meant to keep my arms still and joined in with the game. But if the nurse ever saw us, and she mostly did, she thundered down the ward, yelled at me, put me back in my little coffin and tied my arms and hands down with bandages to the sides of the bed really tight. It was like being crucified flat. There were so many times when I wanted to play and talk and I would wriggle and accidentally break bits off the cast. And this would mean that I had to be replastered. The nurses got really furious and they would quite often wheel me, bed and all, into the cold, wet bathroom as a punishment. And I had to cry myself to sleep to the sound of the dripping tap.

Frequently hospital treatment and operations failed and children returned to their institution in a worse condition than when they arrived.

John Greatorex was born in 1919 in Howden near Goole. At the age of eleven he had an accident whilst playing football which badly damaged his eyes.

When I lost my sight I was put straight into hospital. I don't think they knew quite what to do about me so I just lay there for a few months and you can imagine how I was feeling. Anyway, slowly over that time my eyes started to get a little bit better and I regained some sight. Of course that was wonderful and it gave us all new hopes for what was going to happen to me. Well, after fifteen weeks lying in the bed and my sight coming back a bit then they decided to operate on me. And that was that. The operation spoilt it all. I lost all my sight again. When I came round I knew that what little sight I had had was gone.

The education that the children received was usually very basic, revolving around simple instruction in the three Rs. Since many of the institutions were controlled by religious charities and run by churchmen and women, great emphasis was placed on the importance of religion. It was seen as playing a major role in shaping the character and morality of the children in their care. Disabled children were offered comfort and the hope of salvation in the next life in return for duty and deference in this. Religion was at the heart of the school day, with an insistence on daily religious worship and instruction in many institutions. Regular attendance at the local church and Sunday School was also normally compulsory. However many of the children did not take their daily dose of religion as seriously as the authorities would have wished. To them it often appeared irrelevant and incomprehensible. Ernest Williams, born in 1915, attended Birmingham Royal Institution for the Blind as a boy in the late 1920s.

I wasn't in fear of religion, I don't think I could say that but it exercised a considerable influence over us, there was no doubt, because it was always being drummed into you. They told us that God had visited us with blindness, in his infinite wisdom and mercy. They used to say that in some mysterious way God was only using us for his purpose. Their ardent pursuit of the dictates of religion were never far away. You were always urged to be happy, even though you had nothing because people who had worldly goods to worry about were the really unhappy people. They wanted us to live a life very close to religion as they were teaching it at that time. Strict prayers every morning, a service in the gym every week, with a visiting minister and church. We used to have enormous long sermons in those days, three quarters of an hour was quite standard. I do remember that we used to play a form of knock out whist when we were supposed to be listening to the sermon. We always had our coats spread across our knees and we'd shuffle the cards along the group of us, and whisper the card we'd turned up and play whist that way. And if you declared that you were playing a card that another boy had got, you were considered a rotten fellow.

Some took advantage of church on Sunday to enjoy a rare moment of freedom. If the church was outside the grounds of the institution it was for many the only chance they had to go outside – though of course there would always be some supervision. Mary Baker:

One of the main things about the place was religion. And in the week we used to go to the chapel before we went to school for our hymns and once later in the day. We went to church three times on Sundays. We all had to go in a crocodile and it was quite a walk for us all. And half way up, the old lady that did the linen, used to stop and say, 'Have you changed your knickers today?' And if you hadn't changed them she'd cart you all the way back to change them. When we were in church we didn't listen, we used to sit and throw letters to the choirboys and just play around. We didn't believe in it, we didn't know what it was. It was something that was just drummed down us and so we made fun of it. But matron used to test us the next day on what the vicar had said in his sermon so I used to write down notes in church and we used to read them later in the dormitory so that we would all be able to answer matron's questions even though most of us hadn't been listening at all.

A class in the gymnasium at Elm Court Blind School in 1908. Severely authoritarian teaching methods were standard practice at this time and often instilled fear into blind pupils.

The quality of schooling the children received varied greatly between different types of institution. Generally the best education was given to the blind for it was widely assumed that out of all children with disabilities they had the greatest learning potential. Victorian institutions for the blind had enjoyed some success in teaching pupils using the new method of braille. There was even a kind of public school for the blind – Worcester College, opened in 1866 – which taught fee paying, middle class boys. All this enhanced the status of teaching the blind so that by the first decades of the century some institutions for the blind could attract trained and committed teaching staff. However the severely authoritarian teaching methods which were standard practice at the time often instilled a special fear in pupils without sight. This frequently reduced the effectiveness of the education that was provided for blind children, as Ted Williams remembers.

I took to braille very quickly after I lost my sight. When I was nine and I'd only been there a year, I could read braille books from the library, it came natural to me. And because I was good at it some of the teachers gave me a lot of help. I know I got special lessons from the headteacher. But they were very hard those teachers. Especially the music teacher. Now I desperately wanted to take music lessons and learn to play, but I was just too frightened. Because that music teacher had such a fearsome reputation, he punished the boys so much, I thought I can't do it. And I didn't. Now that was a great opportunity lost, all because the teacher was such a disciplinarian.

There was a growing interest in educating deaf children from the late nineteenth century onwards which brought some advantages in terms of trained teachers and extended schooling. However in most institutions there was a narrow pursuit of the oral method of communication involving lip reading and deaf aids which many children found extremely difficult. Signing – the natural language of the deaf – was often brutally repressed. Joyce Nicholson was a pupil at The Royal School for the Deaf and Dumb, in Birmingham, in the 1920s.

We were never allowed to sign in class at school. They tried to make us speak and to lipread which I really found difficult. We used to look forward to being out of the teacher's eye so we could sign. We used to sign behind their backs when they were writing on the blackboard with our hands under our desks. But if you were caught the teacher would be very angry. Sometimes we would get smacked on the hands and our arms would be tied by our sides for the morning or afternoon just to stop us from signing. One day my teacher caught me signing to my friend under the desk. She was angry and said that I shouldn't use sign. She said that I looked like a little monkey. That's what they used to call us whenever they caught us signing, little monkeys.

The instruction given at institutions for 'physical defectives' or 'cripple schools' was often inferior to the education received by blind and deaf children. There was little knowledge or understanding about how to overcome the difficulties of speech and co-ordination that confronted children with disabilities like cerebral palsy. Too often it was assumed that children like this were 'feeble minded' and were practically ineducable. Also the minimal attempts at instructing these children someimes met with a hostile response from members of the nursing staff who believed that any education was wasted on them. Gerald Turner was sent to Loxley House Home for Crippled Boys in Sheffield in 1942 when he was ten years old from his home in South Yorkshire.

We went out to school three times a week. I really enjoyed it there. It was exciting learning new things because I had never been able to go to school before and I was ten by then so I really did want to learn. They taught us how to write a bit with chalk and to draw, just simple things to start us off like. But as soon as we got back to the home the matron would knock anything we had learnt out of us. It seemed like she didn't think we should be allowed to learn. She wouldn't let us have any books. And if you was caught reading you got a crack behind the ear and the book would be torn up in front of your eyes. Mother and dad didn't know anything about all this going on and when they came to visit me once every month they used to bring me books and comics. They were really pleased that I was going to school at last. Course they didn't know that as soon as they left the matron took all my new books off me and ripped them up.

And when we weren't at school we weren't allowed to do anything except sit around all day until we were put to bed, sometimes at four pm. They just did it to get us out of the way I think. I used to get very bored and frustrated. But none of us boys dared to tell anyone. We were scared of being hit more and we were too weak to run away. I had only just learnt to walk. But I would have run if I could have! I think the lot of them would have, we were that miserable. So at night we lay in the dormitory and dreaded having to get up the next morning. I remember we used to say to each other, 'What will tomorrow bring?'

The level of education provided at orphanages taking in children with physical disabilities was usually equally low. Of the 50,000 children housed in British orphanages in the 1920s around one in ten were disabled in some way, such was the shortage of accommodation for children with disabilities. Although orphanages often provided regular instruction for their able-bodied inmates there was frequently little education given to children with disabilities. More often than not they would be used to do any menial tasks or odd jobs they were thought capable of in the orphanage.

Dennis Smith had contracted polio at the age of three in 1933 and as a result was unable to walk. Soon after this he was sent to The Peabody Home, an orphanage in Warwick, where he was to spend the rest of his childhood.

I never had any schooling all the time I was at the home. If you couldn't get up and walk about to get there yourself then you couldn't go, that was the attitude. Course, I didn't have a chair or anything like that in those days, I just scuffled around on the floor, so it was impossible for me to go to school. They didn't bother much. Just gave me jobs to do in the home. I peeled potatoes, scrubbed floors and chores like that. They thought of any menial duties for me to do while the other kids were in lessons. I was just like an unpaid worker, a skivvy. It was hard for me, but the worst thing was the boredom. I wasn't learning anything, no reading, no writing or stuff you are supposed to get at that age. All I knew was how to peel veg! I know I used to get frustrated and ask all the time if I could go to school with the others but they said it was too difficult to get me there. They just couldn't be bothered so I was stuck in the home, had to do as I was told – so, no school.

A few disabled children in the care of orphanages were exploited even more callously as a source of cheap labour.

From the 1850s onwards many children in orphanages and homes were shipped off to the colonies. It was a cheap way of emptying overcrowded orphanages and providing the Empire with child labour on isolated farmsteads where it was difficult to get workers. Around 90,000 were exported to Canada up to the 1920s, some of whom were disabled.

In 1913 twelve year old Florence Aulph who suffered from a disability in one of her legs was sent to Canada from the Dr Barnardo's Home near Newcastle where she had spent most of her childhood. As with most of these 'lost children of the Empire' she had no choice in the matter. Nobody even told her mother that she was being taken away.

We went down to the docks in carriages drawn by four horses, where the big ship was waiting. We were three weeks crossing and most of us were dreadfully seasick all the way. We landed at Quebec and we then had to go on a small boat down the St Lawrence river and then we went to Peterborough and it was a children's home, a great big building. There were a hundred boys and a hundred girls. They had all our names down in a book and they would take a couple of us in the room at a time and ask us, 'Where would you like to live, in the city or out in a farm?' And stupid me said, 'On a farm'. I did everything the hard way.

And that was the way we were sorted out. And the first place I went to was Hagersville. It was called a foster home, just me and two little boys and they were good to me. I went to school while there for just one year, as I did so want to pass my entrance into high school. And that's as far as I got. There was not much stress put on education as there is today. I never went off the place, only to school. I never played with the other kids, we were just Home kids, and you just weren't supposed to have any feelings. You weren't considered as good as the rest of the kids, because you had no home of your own and no parents.

I was at Hagersville for three years. Then suddenly one day I was picked up, no reason and sent to Fergus. It was a dreadful place. I had a life of hell there. The man had a vicious temper and he used to beat me up if I forgot something or didn't do it right. I was just a bundle of nerves. You see, I was the hired man and the housemaid too. I worked my heart and soul out there for three dollars a month, thirty-six dollars per year. It kept me with something to wear on my feet, that's all, and people threw some of their old clothes at me and I would sit up till midnight, putting a pin here and a pin there; and that's how I learned to sew. I had no money, I couldn't do anything else.

Most orphanage children with physical disabilities however remained in Britain. Canada and Australia really wanted able-bodied children and normally refused children with disabilities. They would also rarely take children from British workhouses. They too were considered 'low grade' and rejected. As late as the 1920s there were still several thousand children housed in workhouses, of which some had physical disabilities. Disabled workhouse children often received virtually no educational instruction at all. They would be used to do cleaning jobs around the workhouse or look after babies and infants on the wards.

Joyce Brayne was born in a workhouse in Warwickshire in 1916. She had cerebral palsy. Her mother left her soon after the birth and Joyce spent the first years of her childhood in the workhouse.

Nobody wanted me because I couldn't walk and I couldn't talk proper. Mother left me in the workhouse and I had to stay there until I was six. We didn't get much food and I had to crawl round on the floor and I slept in a big high bed and I were always scared to fall out. And I had to look after eight babies there when I could feed meself. I tested the bottles of milk on my arm. That was my job and I fed them every four hours. Never learned to write or speak properly because nobody took no notice so long as I did my work. But I were only really little then and I had to do everything I was told or I got smacked.

At the age of six Joyce was removed and placed in the Warwick County Mental Institution. Here she was again given no schooling at all and she was used as a source of free child labour around the hospital.

Then I had to go to the hospital to live. They thought I weren't normal because I couldn't manage to talk to them. At the hospital I had a baby chair to push around in. We never had reading or writing, only hard work and whatever the staff ordered me to do I had to obey. Mostly I had to polish the floors. I sat in me chair and had a big stick with a cloth on the end and great slabs of beeswax. That was hard for me. And I had no friends because all the other residents were dirty and wet themselves. They just thought I were like them but I weren't.

The practice of incarcerating children with physical disabilities in long stay mental handicap hospitals was in fact extremely common during the first half of the century. The medical orthodoxy of the late Victorian and Edwardian years was that physical and mental disabilities were closely related. Many doctors confidently assumed that a mental defect could be detected by physical signs. Consequently children who had difficulties in communicating or in co-ordinating their movements and children who had fits were often labelled as mentally disabled and put away. Often the reality was that they had epilepsy, cerebral palsy, impaired vision or problems with their hearing. If such a child had a physical 'abnormality' like a prominent jaw, an unusually shaped head or a malformation of the ears, this was seen as further evidence of their mental defect.

These children with physical disabilities who were wrongly diagnosed as also being mentally disabled swelled the numbers who were locked up in asylums and mental handicap hospitals at this time. The number of asylums increased from four hundred in the mid-nineteenth century to around 2,000 by 1914. This increase was fuelled by a fear – strongly influenced by the new science of Eugenics – that the mentally disabled were undermining the health and strength of the British nation. They were closely associated in much official thinking with crime, poverty, physical degeneration and sexual immorality. The favoured solution was to segregate them from the rest of society to avoid further contamination. Right up to the 1950s children with physical disabilities continued to be wrongly incarcerated in mental handicap hospitals as a result of these attitudes.

In 1951 at the age of five Evelyn King was admitted to one of the largest mental handicap hospitals in the North of England. She had cerebral palsy which prevented her from walking or from speaking more than a few words. After failing an intelligence test administered by doctors she was diagnosed as 'an imbecile' who was unfit to be educated. In fact Evelyn had all her mental faculties, she simply had great difficulty in speaking.

When I first came I was in a baby wheelchair. I never used to walk and I couldn't talk. And I weren't happy here as a girl 'cos it was a bit miserable, you know. On the villa we played dominoes, ludo and snap cards and I played jigsaws and did sewing. I used to get a little bit bored and I used to look out of the window and dream about me poor mum and dad – 'cos I never used to go home and I missed all that. Then later on I started school but I only had school in the morning, not in the afternoon. And the staff, they were very strict. We had to be careful what *of the told Patient.*

Dated the ___12th___ day of ___May___ 19_51_

To the Board of Control.

———————

MEDICAL STATEMENT.

I have this day (* ___12th May,1951___) examined the above-named

Patient and HEREBY CERTIFY that the Mental Condition of the Patient is as follows:—†

She is an Imbecile. She fails to name common objects, to indicate objects by their use and to copy a circle. She has a mental age of 2 years by Terman-Merrill tests.

and h___ Bodily Health and Condition are as follows:—

She is in poor health and suffers from cerebral diplegia with a history of epilepsy.

After failing an intelligence test at the age of five Evelyn King was classified as an imbecile and admitted to one of the largest mental handicap hospitals in the North of England.

we said in them days. Once I got upset, you know and I just got hold of this stick and threw it. And the window cracked. Didn't go right through, just cracked. And they asked me why I did it and I said 'cos someone upset me. I told them why I did it because I was upset. And I got punished for that, couldn't do nothing. It was boring and if you didn't get any visitors then you sat in the day room and people used to shout and things.

Children with physical disabilities were widely perceived as a kind of inferior species. In an age which celebrated the virtues of a healthy body and a healthy mind – and which believed there was a close connection between the two – they appeared to be less than human. These feelings of disgust and horror towards the child inmates found graphic expression in a range of harsh punishments that were inflicted upon them. Many were routinely punished for minor misdemeanours. This was the ultimate deterrent which aimed to instill unquestioning obedience in the children. Evelyn King:

Sometimes I were just a bit frightened because they'd get right strict and funny with you, you know. Just had to keep your mouth shut. But we used to just get punished and everything. And I remember as well, when we used to scrub floors, when we were naughty, if we were rude to the staff or anything like. We used to be scrubbing floors all day long. Couldn't go out anywhere. Right punish. We used to be locked inside our rooms, locked doors and the boys used to be in their pyjamas and the girls used to be in their nightdresses. And you used to scrub floors all day, and it wasn't very nice. Everyone looked fed up and browned off 'cos they couldn't do what they would like. And I used to be scared stiff. And I remember I couldn't use a knife and fork then. I can now, but I never used to. I used to use a spoon and if I spilt something, like tea, they used to get a cloth and make me wipe it up. I used to say, 'I'm sorry, I did it on accident.' But they still made you wipe it up, because I did it see. Sometimes they would say, 'If you do this again, you won't see your mothers and fathers again, I won't have this.' So we had to be careful what we say to them. I didn't like it in them days, when they used to be strict. I hated some of them, yes. I didn't like it, it used to make you upset, you know.

Although this was an era when corporal punishment was widely used in schools, the punishments inflicted upon children with disabilities were of an altogether different order. The most brutal aspect of these punishments was that they often actively exploited the children's disabilities. A variety of mental and physical tortures were used in many institutions, designed to humiliate and terrify the most defiant young inmates. Ted Williams remembers the brutal punishments used at Manchester Road School for the Blind in the 1920s.

One of the prevalent methods of caning was on the hand. Blind people, of course, are very dependent on their hands and fingers but I suffered a stroke hard across the fingers quite often. And believe you me it used to hurt. Well, that for quite a while left the hand really numb and dead and we used to have to wait before we could even think about looking at a braille book, until the numbness wore off. One particular teacher used to delight in punishing us in the maths lesson. We all had little arithmetic frames with sharp points sticking up to denote certain numbers to us. Now, if the teacher was trying to instill a sum into our heads and we couldn't get it she would clamp her hands on the backs of our fingers on these points and press them down and say, 'Can't you feel? Can't you feel?' And this again meant our fingers would be dead for a good time afterwards and any braille reading was impossible. The punishment that the teachers used to concentrate on though was Coventry. At the smallest offence you could be put into Coventry. Now, that meant that you must not speak, except to a teacher, for the period they stated. And what made it worse the other children must not speak to you, otherwise they got the same punishment. Many's the time when I was caught for speaking out of turn or bumping into another boy in line and that was that, – 'Williams, was that you? You can have two days in Coventry.' Once I was punished for something that two of us had done and the other boy got off. Part of my punishment was Coventry and in spite of myself, everywhere I went I were saying, 'It's beastly unfair, it's unfair.' And a teacher heard me so I got punished again for talking and my Coventry was extended. Another day's silence for me. Well, I was a bit of a loner and I could take refuge in reading and, more or less studying and making poetry up, and I would get in a corner of a desk in the playroom and keep myself to myself. But to some of the children, who were the merry kind of boys and who couldn't read, then a time in Coventry was absolutely dreadful. That punishment was the one we hated most, imagine as a blind person, being shut off from your main way of getting about and communicating, it was worse than getting the cane for us boys.

This kind of sensory deprivation was especially common in institutions which contained both blind and deaf children housed in separate wings. Disobedient blind children would be sent to the deaf section and vice versa. Cyril Hayward Jones was a pupil at The Mount School for the Deaf and the Blind near Stoke-on-Trent around the time of the First World War.

There was one side of the building for us blind boys and the other side was for deaf boys. One of the worst punishments was to go and live on the deaf side for a couple of days. If we talked in the dining room or some such little misdemeanour they could hand out that punishment. That was the only time we ever went to the deaf side, when we were naughty. Now the thing was, of course, that the deaf couldn't hear and we couldn't lip read. So it was a really pretty desperate situation there. Well, what you had to do was learn to spell on your fingers, to be able to make yourself understood with the deaf boys, I remember the manual alphabet even to this day. We used to take the deaf boy's hand and spell out the words on his hand. Without that we would have been completely cut off from the world, in absolute silence.

Often no pity was shown to children who cried. This was also to be punished for it broke the elaborate rules that insisted upon silence for much of the day. Jeanne Hollamby:

At first when my mum took me into hospital when I was five she said that she would be coming back soon to take me home. She was just trying to be nice but when she didn't come I started crying and crying. So one of the nurses put me into a small room, sort of a toy cupboard. It was really dark and I could feel things crawling over my legs and I screamed until someone came to find me and when they opened the door there were cockroaches all over the floor.

In a few institutions any children who broke the rules on silence in the dormitory would be sadistically victimised. Bryan Dive:

I remember one time after lights out – that was at seven o'clock – I was whispering to my mate. The staff used to creep around listening out for our voices and that time they caught me. They got me out of bed, put my dressing gown on and took me out into the corridor in between the two dormitories. Then I had to stand in the middle of the corridor for half an hour on my own. It hurt me a lot because I can't stand on my own because of my legs. I had to concentrate hard and I tried to hold onto the wall. They knew I couldn't stand without a chair but they made me do it.

Bed wetting was also often a punishable offence. It was a common problem caused principally by the atmosphere of fear and anxiety that the children lived in. In addition dormitory regulations which often prevented the children from leaving their beds at night and difficulties resulting from the children's physical disabilities all made the problem worse. The reaction of some members of staff to constantly soiled sheets was extremely brutal. Marjorie Jacques:

I used to wet the bed a lot when I was little. Now they wouldn't let you have potties, they didn't allow those. If I wanted to go in the night and I woke up I used to have to crawl out of bed, right down the hallway and drag myself up onto the toilet, see. But mainly I couldn't get myself out of bed because of my legs and I used to just wet the bed. In the mornings we used to have to strip our beds and the nurse would come around to inspect them. If it was wet you were in trouble. I used to dread that inspection because, of course, mine was quite often wet because it was so difficult for me to get myself out of bed. The punishment for wetting was one I really hated. They made me knit a pair of black stockings on four needles, with a seam right up the back. And if you made a mistake then you had to unpick it and start again. I knitted God knows how many pairs of stockings with me wetting the bed a few times a week. I think now that it was because I was so homesick. I was only three and a half when I was first sent there. Anyway, every night after school I would have to go up to my dormitory to do these stockings. They would bring up my tea, one piece of bread and treacle. I had to sit all on my own trying to knit and feeling pretty lonely and miserable. Another punishment for bedwetting was to take things away from us. I remember once my mum sent me a lovely birthday cake and they wouldn't let me have it 'cos I'd been naughty, I'd wet the bed or something probably. They put it in a store room and locked the door. But when they got it out two days later it was full of ants so it had to just be thrown away.

The opportunities for children to resist such a harsh system of control and punishment were extremely limited. They were under immense psychological pressure to obey the rules at all times. Nevertheless most former inmates of institutions remember some acts of defiance. They seem to have been important in maintaining a personal as opposed to an institutional identity. Sometimes this resistance took the form of a symbolic gesture. Children would for example refuse to cry or show remorse or admit guilt when they were unfairly punished, thus winning a moral victory over the institution. Ernest Williams:

I got six of the best for failing an exam once. It was a maths exam, I remember and I didn't get very adequate marks. And the view was that you were expected to do as well as they assessed you were capable of doing and I didn't do that. So I got six in front of the junior school. Six on the backside. I was really angry about it because I didn't think I deserved it. And the one thing that I was determined to do was that I would not cry. I'd seen other fellows howl their heads off but I decided I wouldn't do it. So I stuck it out and it was very painful. And that made the master that gave me the six very angry. I can remember him doing his best to make me cry and on the fifth and sixth stroke he came down much harder. But I wouldn't cry. And afterwards he said, 'Now you boys, I had to give Williams the cane and you needn't think he came out of it a hero, he didn't. He went very pale and he trembled very much, so don't imagine that he was a hero.' And that was him trying to get equal, having failed to make me howl.

The resistance frequently revolved around stealing food. The children were often hungry as the meals provided were very basic. And there were no second helpings for those with big appetites. The last meal of the day was usually 'tea' around five o'clock, after which no food was given to the children for the rest of the day. Many remember going to bed very hungry as a result. The children would spend hours illicitly plotting how to get extra food, most of which would be hidden and secretly eaten in the dormitory. Vegetable patches and orchards inside the grounds of the institution were often the main target for these 'crimes'. Ted Williams:

Some of us children who showed an aptitude for it were told to go and clear this patch, rhubarb patch at the top of the girls' grounds, and I was one of them. So when we were gardening I listened out for the overseer being not around and I kept sneaking sticks of rhubard. And I pushed two or three down my jumper and two or three down my shirt and I spent the rest of the day with my arm pressed against my stomach so that they wouldn't show. Anyway I did manage to get through to bed time. And I got them up to the dormitory and I got this rhubarb and my word I didn't half wolf it down, terrific. Well, I ate it all except one stick, and I left that under me pillow while next morning. When I went and got washed I did manage to get the rhubarb pushed under me shirt again, to wait for playtime for a time to eat it. Later in the morning I was walking across the boys' square, and I've still got this stick of rhubarb, holding it with me arm, and the idea was to go into the boys' lavatory across the square and eat it. Well I was half way across the square when suddenly a figure steps up in front of me and I hear a funny sound. And I said, 'Hello who are you?' And a voice said, 'Very nice, very nice Williams'. And do you know, the rhubarb had worked up out of me shirt and the end was sticking up out and this teacher in front of me was stood chomping the top off. He reported me and so I got an hundred and fifty lines, 'I must not steal rhubarb'.

Often the secret raids were organised by groups of children or even the whole dormitory. Mary Baker:

Our playground was near to the orchard and we used to go over the bridge. It was a bit rickety but still we used to go and we had someone shying for us, guarding in case matron came. We used to go down the orchard and there used to be pears down there, beautiful pears and apples. We used to stuff these down our knickers, as many as we could. At one time we had a girl with a peg leg. It was hollow so she would take it off for us to fill with apples. Then we would wobble back to the playroom or the dormitory and hand them round. If anyone came we used to take the cores and wrap them up in bits of paper so that they wouldn't notice what was put in the bin. We were never found out anyway or there would have been a lot of trouble.

At the Yorkshire Institution for the Deaf the raids on the school orchard were organised by the prefects, as Dennis Boucher remembers.

When I was about thirteen or fourteen at my school the boys were always hungry. Anyway the prefect, he used to make me and three or four other boys go scrumping apples or pears. There was loads of trees next to the school. So we used to crawl at night, when it was quite dark, come right into the orchard, into the field and pinch all these apples, fill our pockets up. And the prefect would say, 'Have you got your pockets full? Yes, have you got enough in your pockets?' Then he'd make us give up all the apples. We would say that we didn't have any more but we would secretly keep two or three back for ourselves. The prefect would hand them out. And then we'd go back to our rooms and eat all these apples and pears. But next morning, God, my stomach. We used to get terrible stomach ache. It was awful. We used to say that we'd never pinch apples again. But we would be back there the next night.

The most daring and dramatic raids were those that involved breaking into the kitchens at night and stealing the food. Mary Baker:

We didn't have enough to eat, so we used to go into the larder late at night. There was a small window that I was able to get in through and we would raid the larder, picking up bits of bread and anything we could put on it – mostly dripping. Then we would scramble back and hide it in our beds and so we could have a good old feasts together.

Very occasionally the children would protest about the food that was served up itself. In 1913 ten year old Cyril Hayward Jones was one of the leaders of a short lived food strike at The Mount School for the Deaf and Blind.

The meals were horrible, usually looked as though it was the leavings say from the week before. We all naturally hated the stuff. Just before the First World War they gave us margarine for the first time. We used to have butter, originally. None of us liked the margarine, it had a horrible fishy taste then so we decided to have a good strike, you see. And we refused to eat. I remember we all sat there not eating and tipping our chairs to and fro and making a noise. Of course, because of the silence rule in the dining room all this noise created a terrible to do. And to top it all quite suddenly my chair tipped backwards and I fell back with it. The master came up. He was absolutely furious at the strike and all the trouble we were causing, he didn't bother about whether I was all right or not, whether I'd bumped my head. He shouted at me and kicked me out, 'Lose two marks'. And that was the end of our strike.

The few school strikes that did occur were usually protests against excessive punishments. Ted Williams recalls one such strike at Manchester Road School for the Blind in Sheffield in 1929.

It had to be something fierce for us to get the courage to really rebel because of the tremendous discipline in the school. Well, there was once a really popular boy in our class, Arthur Hayes, a grand personality. One of the teachers punished him for something he said and us boys all knew that he had not done. And, well, the teacher accused and punished him but all us boys, his friends and mates, stood by him. We organised a strike. We just refused to work in class. We sat there with our arms folded and wouldn't lift a finger. It was all against the injustice of the thing. Even in the music class we all refused to sing. Of course, we all got punished severely for striking and after a couple of days we were forced to give in to the teachers.

The most dramatic and dangerous form of resistance was the escape attempt. In the eyes of the institutional authorities this was the most serious of all offences which was to be punished accordingly. Cyril Hayward Jones remembers an extraordinary escape attempt of blind boys eager to do their bit for King and Country which occurred at the Mount School in 1915.

During the First World War a lot of the workers from the school were called up into the army and us boys felt as though we should do our bit too. One of the boys suggested that we run away and said he had an uncle with a farm not very far from the school. The idea was that we would help with the war effort on the farm, although what we could have done I don't know. At the time we thought it a grand idea and we fixed it all up. And so one night we crept down the stairs after everyone had gone to bed and set out by climbing out of one of the windows. We were thrilled to bits and we wandered around the lanes after this boy, because he had a bit of sight. We went quite a way and at last we found a farm that he thought was it. We went down the yard and a window opened. Then a voice calls out, 'Who are you?' Well, it turned out that it wasn't this uncle's farm, we'd gone the wrong way. So all we could do was to go back. We got back to school and we thought we'd got away with it. But next morning we were called to the headmaster. Apparently the gardener had seen us getting back into school. So the punishment was that we had to go and live on the deaf side. And we had to hand our trousers in to the senior deaf boy every night so that we shouldn't run away again. That was an immense humiliation.

When children escaped it was often assumed by members of staff that many other inmates had conspired in the plan. They were then also to be severely punished, partly in the hope that they would provide information on the whereabouts of the children who had absconded. Ted Williams:

There were two boys here that ran away one Saturday morning. There was a right hoo-ha. But what was astounding was that they punished all the school, all the boys, because they had run away. I don't know how on earth it concerned us boys. But the teachers claimed that we should have stopped them running away. Well, we didn't know they'd run away for two or three hours afterwards. But the teacher came into the playroom and admonished us for not preventing them from running away and put us all in Coventry. She said that we would all be in Coventry until the boys were brought back. Lucky for us these two boys were collared by the police around tea time.

Very few children were successful in their escape attempts. They were hindered by their disability which often slowed them down. Their uniform was also a problem as it made them very conspicuous and likely to be arrested. They often had no money to buy food and to travel. And they were usually ignorant of the local geography for many institutions were located in country areas a long way from where the children originally lived.

The most effective way for children to escape from their institutions was in fact to alert their parents to what was actually happening to them. The control and censorship that was exercised over any communication with the outside world made this very difficult. Marjorie Jacques was one of the few who found a way to defeat this system.

Marjorie Jacques (right) with her older sister in the 1930s. Marjorie had to smuggle letters out to her family to let them know about the terrible conditions at the Chailey Heritage Institution where she was an inmate.

Every Tuesday during school lessons we were allowed to write home. They didn't trust you to put the letter in the envelope. They had to read all our letters first to make sure that we didn't tell our parents what a bad time we were having. Now as I got older I got craftier. I used to be really good for the teacher so that she let me put my letter in the envelope on my own. I used to quickly scribble on the bottom of the letter what was happening at Chailey, all the punishments and things like putting sticking plaster over our mouths if we talked. That's how my parents started to realise how unhappy I was. Anyway, the next Christmas I landed back at home wearing boots that were two sizes too small for me. My big toe was all doubled up and I had broken septic chilblains all up to my knees and on my thighs. Of course, my parents decided that that was it, I wasn't going back. They had to get special permission from the education authority to take me back home. I thought that was wonderful. I'd never been so happy.

CHAPTER FOUR
INDECENT BEHAVIOUR

In 1926 eleven year old Ernest Williams was an inmate of the St. Helen's Institution for the Blind in Swansea. One Sunday he innocently fell victim to the institution's rigid rules on the segregation of the sexes.

We had to go to Sunday school every week and we'd file in crocodiles with a line of boys next to a line of girls. One Sunday one of the girls shouted out, 'Ernest Williams touched my knickers'. I'd bumped into her accidentally as I was walking but I hadn't done anything to her. That was it. I was reported and there was an unholy row. The next morning I was reprimanded in front of the whole school in the hall. I remember I was called out to the front and the headmistress said, 'You're worse than the beasts in the field, isn't it boy?' I was angry because I hadn't done anything and I wouldn't admit to it. I suppose I would have been wiser to have cried and given in. But I remember the authorities couldn't decide what the best punishment was for my wickedness. They were going to thrash me. Eventually I remember a man saying, 'Put him away until he cleanses himself.' I was locked in the sick room in solitary confinement with a bread and water diet. I was given nothing to read. I kept myself going by inventing games in my head. And the kitchen maid – Gwynneth her name was – she helped me too. She must have felt sorry for me because she used to sneak up with a pear or a bar of chocolate from the kitchen. I know once she gave me a big hug and I felt her tears splashing down on the side of my face. Then after what seemed about four days they let me out. I still hadn't confessed but they said that Lord Jesus Christ had taken it into his heart to forgive me and my wicked ways and so they could take me back into the school again.

Boys and girls were rigorously kept apart in institutions for physically disabled people. Often they would be brought up in separate institutions altogether or in segregated wings of the same building. At the very least there would normally be separate entrances and separate playgrounds, often divided by high walls or fences to prevent any casual contact between the sexes. This

(Opposite above) *A Dr. Barnardo's institution for boys in the 1900s. Boys and girls were rigorously kept apart in institutions for physically disabled people. Often they would be brought up in separate institutions altogether.*

(Opposite below) *An institution for deaf children in the 1940s. Classes were strictly segregated and even the slightest contact between boys and girls would be punished.*

segregation was to some extent a reflection of broader social attitudes which approved of keeping boys and girls apart in schooling and leisure activities. The dominant educational theories before the last war for example claimed that single sex schools were very advantageous in avoiding potentially dangerous contact between the sexes at a vulnerable age.

However there was a special concern, which often verged on obsession, with segregating the sexes in institutions for disabled people. There was a traditional assumption amongst the religious charities and Poor Law officials who controlled many of these institutions that certain types of disabled people were highly promiscuous and fertile. In particular women classified as 'feeble-minded' were seen as slaves to their animal passions and were thus supposedly a moral danger to the community. These stereotypes which closely linked moral and physical 'degeneracy' were strongly reinforced in the early part of the century by the new and fashionable science of Eugenics. Eugenists often represented disabled people as helpless, ignorant or insane. They claimed that mental and physical disability was an hereditary problem passed on through so-called defective families. This 'bad stock' was thought to be undermining the strength and efficiency of the British race because people with disabilities were reproducing at a much faster rate than the able-bodied. This reproduction of the 'unfit' was thought to be one of the main causes of the poverty, unemployment, criminality, alcoholism and idleness which preoccupied many Edwardian social reformers.

An image taken from the Eugenics film Heredity in Man *in 1937. The Eugenics movement often represented disabled people as helpless, ignorant or insane.*

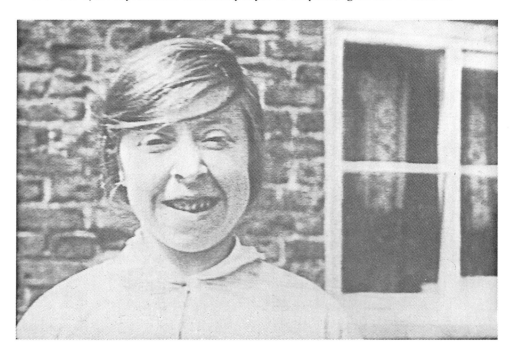

The day room for young women in a mental handicap hospital in the 1930s. Sex segregation was most rigid in mental handicap hospitals and colonies.

The Eugenist solution was to prevent disabled people from reproducing, or at least dramatically reduce their rate of reproduction, thereby maintaining racial purity. Eugenist ideas like these were less influential in Britain than in America where sterilisation was common or in Nazi Germany where there was first a mass programme of sterilisation followed by the extermination of around a quarter of a million disabled people. In Britain sterilisation was never officially adopted as a policy because it was widely believed that it would encourage promiscuity and the spread of venereal disease – then a major problem – by taking away the fear of pregnancy. The main strategy to curb the fertility of the 'unfit' was sex segregation. It was pursued with extraordinary vigour in almost all institutions where disabled people lived.

Eugenist ideas strongly influenced the passing of the Mental Defectives Act in 1913 which gave local authorities far reaching powers to place people having sex outside of marriage into institutions. Those most vulnerable to victimisation under this legislation were disabled people or young men and women with learning difficulties. Many found themselves classified as moral imbeciles and were locked away in long stay mental handicap hospitals, sometimes for the rest of their lives.

Sex segregation was in fact most rigid in mental handicap hospitals and colonies. This was partly because they often housed people who had broken the narrow sexual mores of the time and were supposed to need close policing. But more important, the authorities were concerned that people with supposed mental disabilities should not be allowed to reproduce. They were seen as the lowest grade of institutional inmate and the most dangerous threat to racial purity. Thus strenuous efforts were made in mental handicap hospitals to ensure that there were no opportunities for uncontrolled encounters or relationships with the opposite sex. This segregation remained very strong even into the post-war years. Evelyn King grew up in a mental handicap hospital in Leeds and remembers the strict segregation rules which existed there.

> Years ago we daren't talk to the boys. Oh no, we had to keep away from them. We didn't even look at them. Girls used to be on one side and boys on the other. If we talked to the boys, you could get in real trouble. I did get frightened to get into trouble for what I say to the boys. So I just kept my mouth shut.

Institutions for physically disabled people had elaborate rules banning any contact or conversation between the sexes. These rules were backed up by severe punishments. Even contact that was completely accidental would often be punished. Ted Williams was an inmate of the Royal Manchester Road School for the Blind in the 1920s.

> The sex segregation at the Blind school was something terrific. We would go back to school in January and we weren't supposed to speak to any girl until we went on holiday in July. Now there were fifty odd boys and thirty odd girls and if ever accidentally we had some sort of contact with a girl, we were actually punished. I myself had the cane for accidentally putting my hand out and feeling at a girl's back more or less to find out who was in front of me in the queue.

Sometimes drugs and sedatives were used to control the behaviour of those who frequently broke the rules on talking to the opposite sex. Owen Weight – born with cerebral palsy in 1922 – spent much of his life in Leasden Mental Institution.

> They separated us from all the girls. Different places we could be and that. You got watched all the time. Some of them did talk to a girl and then they got punished always. They got a sleeping draught or a needle

in their arm and that was really bad. They used to do that to us to keep us still and so we didn't talk very much.

In tandem with this attempt to prevent any contact between the sexes went an offensive against the evils of masturbation. It was assumed in many institutions that the inmates would turn to 'self-abuse' or the 'solitary vice' to find sexual relief and pleasure. Staff often became obsessed with the idea that these secret vices were widely practised in common rooms and dormitories. Their concern was partly rooted in the moral and medical panic that masturbation had a seriously damaging effect on the mind and the body. With very little evidence many clergymen, doctors and psychiatrists writing around the turn of the century argued that excessive masturbation was a major cause of many diseases and disabilities such as blindness, epilepsy and even insanity. Professor G. Stanley Hall, the world's leading authority on adolescence described self-abuse in 1911 as an 'insidious disease', 'the scourge of the human race' and 'an influence that seems to spring from the Prince of Darkness'. Many staff seem to have believed that masturbation was not only morally degrading the inmates, it was also aggravating their disabilities. The habit was thought to be most widespread amongst boys but large numbers of girls were also believed to be infected. This masturbation paranoia seems to have been greatest in institutions for the blind. Former inmates remember constant accusations and purges. Ted Williams:

There was a mania with masturbation, the teachers thought we were at it all the time. They were most suspicious when we were in the dormitory because all the boys were locked in together every night. Well one night a friend of mine put a sheet over his head and crept up on me and whispered in a spooky voice, 'I'm a ghost'. I knew it was him and we had a friendly fight, rolling around under the blankets together, laughing. The teacher who was patrolling outside the dormitory must have heard the noise. 'Williams, Johnson, see me tomorrow morning'. We didn't think we were in serious trouble because we had no idea of what he suspected us of. Anyway when we reported to him in the morning he said, 'You'd better come into the washroom. Now I want both of you to undo your trousers and show me what you did to each other last night. Williams was it you who started this orgy?' I had no idea what he meant. Then he encouraged us to touch each other. My friend admitted to it so he got off lightly, but I refused, I wouldn't tell a lie. But I came off worst. I had to write, 'I must not be rude to myself' three hundred times and he sent a letter about the incident to my father. The worst thing was I was sent to Coventry, nobody was allowed to speak to me in the school for three days.

Ernest Williams remembers a similar paranoia about masturbation at the Birmingham Royal Institution for the Blind where he was transferred in 1927.

We had one master in particular who was always sneaking around in my view looking for boys to nab for masturbating. Anyway one night in the dormitory he called my name out and told me to come with him into the bathroom. He shut the door and then said to me, 'You've been abusing yourself haven't you boy? Don't protest, I saw you.' Then quite suddenly he said to me, 'You've still got a fair amount of sight haven't you Williams?' And I said that I had. 'You want to keep your sight don't you? Well, you're going the right way to losing it, aren't you?' And from that I was to assume that if you masturbate you would go blind.

Most of the children and young people in institutions were kept in total ignorance about the facts of life. There was normally no sex instruction at all, even of the rudimentary type which began in some state schools during the first half of the century. Menstruation was treated as a secret source of shame. The most common advice given to disabled girls in institutions was to hide their guilty secret and to avoid boys whenever they had a period. All this produced a high level of anxiety and fear in which sexual myths flourished. Mary Baker spent her adolescence at Halliwick Home for Crippled Girls in North London in the 1930s.

When we became women we used to have the degradedness of going up to a cupboard to get out sanitary towels. Before my periods started I used to wonder what was the girls standing at the cupboard for? We weren't told anything and all the younger girls used to titter 'cos we weren't sure what was happening. But one morning I found a stain on my sheets and I told one of the nurses and she told me to go to the cupboard. You used to sign on at the cupboard in this little book and we used to be able to go to get towels three times a day. And these had to last you whether you were losing a lot or a little, you just had to have those. And sometimes they really stank because you only got clean clothes once a week, so your knickers were only clean once a week. They were really horrible. And you always had this feeling that somebody else could smell you, 'cos you could smell it on your own clothes. And when you'd finished and say maybe a day later you had a little trickle again you couldn't go back and get another towel because you were booked out again until next month. But we had no inkling of how our bodies were changing and what it meant. All we were told was that it was something that wasn't needed in our bodies and that we wouldn't have to talk to any boys, because now we were women. But the other side, the sex side, we didn't understand at all, we weren't taught about it. We had no idea what the consequences would be. All we knew was if we kissed we might have babies.

The elaborate institutional rules on dress which normally insisted on uniforms, regulation hair cuts and which banned any form of self-adornment

The Halliwick Home for Crippled Girls in London pictured in the 1930s. The elaborate institutional rules on dress meant that many young disabled people developed a negative self-image.

meant that many young disabled people developed a negative self-image. Some girls and young women secretly tried to make themselves as attractive as possible but the staff in most institutions did their upmost to ensure that the inmates appearance conformed to a chaste and asexual stereotype. Jeanne Hollamby was sent to Halliwick when she was sixteen in 1939.

When I first got to Halliwick they gave me a bath and my hair was cut really short, up around my ears. I was sixteen and so I was really a young woman by then but the nurses said none of us girls were allowed to wear bras. They seemed to want us all to stay really young and plain. They didn't think we had the same feelings as other girls who are growing up. We weren't allowed to make outselves look nice at all. We had to keep our hair very straight and any make up was absolutely banned. We had to pay for soap and toothpowder out of our little bit of pocket money. We used to use toothpowder to polish our nails, but that was about as far as our vanity could go. The worst thing I thought was that we were only allowed one clean pair of knickers every week. What I used to do was to wash them in the sink secretly at night and dry them by putting them under my mattress and sleeping on them all night. Every little thing was denied us. Even when my sister got married I was only allowed out to the wedding for a few hours. Of course I was really looking forward to it. My mum had got me a nice dress to wear and as a special treat I went to a hairdresser's and had my hair Marcel waved. That was all the rage then and so I thought I looked great. But as soon as the wedding was over I had to go straight back to Halliwick. And the minute I got back they whisked me off into the bathroom to be scrubbed and have all my hair pulled straight again.

However some of the inmates managed to find a way around the rules. Love letters were the most common form of secret communication between girls and boys. Mary Baker:

The only time we ever saw boys our own age was in the choir at church every Sunday. So we used to write little notes and screw them up and throw them up at them. I was interested in a boy called Smiley. So I wrote a note that just said, 'I love you Smiley, from Mary'. Of course we didn't really know what love meant but we used to send soppy things up. Whether they received them was a different thing but we believed they did because they used to smile at us when we used to sort of make eyes at them. It was just a vision that we thought we'd love to be with the boys. If we'd have got caught we really would have got a good telling off or gone without something. But luckily we were never caught.

Grace was born in 1915 and attended a special school until she was fourteen. After attempting to commit suicide, which was then illegal, she was placed in a mental handicap hospital at the age of eighteen. She remembers how the inmates tried to get around the strict rules of segregation.

I did cabbage you see. And love letters were sent through cabbages; used to fold them up. They used to cut 'em in half, cabbages, and stick it together again. And when the boys came in with their pot of tea in the morning, there used to always be a letter underneath. They could've got on bloomin' villa eight (punishment villa) for months and months if they were found out. They used to say, 'Don't tell 'em.' And I never told, poor lasses.

The sending of love letters was often viewed as a serious breach of discipline and anyone caught would usually be severely punished. Ted Williams:

Now when we had classes, on one side was the girls and on the other side the boys. Well there was a girl there that when she spoke, oh my word, I just, I really fancied her and I found that in classes she sat at the first girl's desk that I had to pass to get to mine. So now, I thought of a brilliant idea of writing a braille letter and as I passed the end of this desk I would shove it into her hand, hoping to God the sighted teacher didn't see it. That in itself was a daredevil thing to do. So, I wrote this letter and I put some funny things like 'darling'. Anyway, it was a schoolboy's love letter and this particular morning I walked past the desk, felt quickly for the girl's hand and shoved this braille letter under it and then clamped her hand down on it. But that morning for the first time in months and months the teacher had swapped the girl's round and so it wasn't the girl I fancied at all who got the letter. And to make it worse this girl gave the letter into the teacher. You wouldn't imagine the palaver I went through for that. I had to apologise to everyone added to a couple of strokes on the hand with the cane and a ten minute lecture on the wickedness of doing such things.

In some cases girls and boys who wrote love letters would be threatened with expulsion. Cyril Hayward-Jones went to the Mount School for the Deaf and Blind in Stoke-on-Trent around the time of the First World War.

We never had any contact with the girls except for prayers, they were absolutely separate from us. There was what we called the 'separation door' and there was tremendous enthusiasm for trying to talk to the girls through the door. The headmaster tended to interpret the most innocent things as signs of guilt. When a boy was seen talking to a girl, he thought it was some sort of intrigue and he took a very serious view of it. I remember once when I was fourteen I met a girl – she was sighted – at chapel. Her name was Muriel, and we spent a little time together, and I decided to write her a letter. I wrote it in braille and I was going to dictate it to one of the housemaids – she'd write it for me, you see. I remember it ended 'your passionate admirer'. I'd only seen the girl once! Well, I left this letter hanging around and a member of staff found it and, of course, I was called before the headmaster. He asked me did I kiss the girl and he wanted to know all the details. I think he got a certain sexual pleasure out of it himself. He was very cross with me; he threatened to expel me and said I was 'an unmitigated blackguard'. He said it was 'the foulest record in the annals of the school', that was for kissing a girl! I was so innocent I didn't know one end of a girl from the other. He sent for my father and I remember my father saying, 'Work, work my son, and regain the confidence of your masters.'

The inmates often had secret meeting places in the grounds of the institution where relationships between older boys and girls could develop. Ernest Williams:

We used to contrive to meet sometimes, in a place called the cookery. It was sort of generally known that you could meet a girl secretly in the cookery while the teaching staff were at supper. But it was taboo and you could be suspended for having a relationship with a girl, for even talking to a girl. You could be sent away from school because it just wasn't allowed. They were afraid, you see, that if we got within striking distance of each other the wrong thing would happen.

In institutions for deaf people signing was frequently used as a kind of secret language, out of sight of the staff, to arrange illicit meetings. Dennis and Hazel Boucher first met at The Yorkshire Residential Institution for the Deaf in the 1930s.

There was a big wall in the playground, separating the girls from the boys and so if I wanted to speak to Hazel or meet up and have a little kiss and cuddle I would ask one of the lads to stand so I could stand on his shoulders and look over the wall and sign for Hazel. So we would pass on secret signs like that. And if the teacher came into sight then we would get down quickly. If the teacher stayed in the playground then we could sneak upstairs to one of the upstairs windows. That way we could look out on the whole playground, even over the wall into the girls' yard. That way we could sign through the window at the girls and make arrangements to meet. There were places we could meet when the teachers were busy. It was quite easy for the girls to nip across to the cloakrooms and so we used to meet there. Just have a kiss and a cuddle in one of the wardrobes, shut the door in case one of the teachers came by. And there was another one, the air raid shelters that we had then. That was the best there because of course nobody ever used them unless there was a raid! Teachers would never think of looking in there. Sometimes we used to make an arrangement and there would already be another boy and girl there so we used to have to have a system of booking the wardrobe or the air shelter so we could take it in turns.

Young people often remained in institutions until their late teens or early twenties and at around this age relationships between inmates were much more likely to become sexual. Nevertheless sexual ignorance, lack of opportunity and the terror of detection meant that few couples risked sexual intercourse. Where sex did take place it was most likely to occur outside the walls of the institution when older inmates took advantage of the occasional privilege of an afternoon or an evening out. Ernest Williams:

I got involved in a relationship with a girl when I was still at school. She had been at my school but then she left and went to live back with her parents. They lived in a pub which her parents were running and I used to go and visit her. I used to have to escape over the wall of the school and feel my way along to where she lived. Then we could sit and talk together and listen to music or something. And it was that way, above the pub, that I was introduced to the sex act. The location was perfect

An institutional dance just after the First World War. At events like these men were normally only allowed to dance with female members of staff or other men.

for being alone you see because everyone was busy downstairs in the bar. But the thing I remember most about it was that I was always haunted by the fact that she might be pregnant and then my secret would be out at the school. It never ceased to worry me until I knew it was all right. And I always used to say, 'I'll never do that again.' But that's not very easy to stick to! If anybody had found out it would have been disastrous for me. It would have been expulsion and goodness knows what else.

The authorities were aware that the most fertile area for sexual relationships was between inmates and those who had recently left. Consequently they frequently tried to ban these relationships – even if they were innocent – as Hazel Boucher remembers.

After Dennis left school I had another year or so to go but we still wanted to see each other. He went off working in Lincoln and so he wrote me a letter. It was a love letter and he sent it to me via a friend of his who was coming to school to visit. But anyway this friend's mum got hold of the letter and she opened it and read it and took it to our headmaster. So the first I knew was that the headmaster came to get me out of one of my classes. I wondered what I had done wrong. He took me into his office and shut the door, it was all very stern. He showed me the letter and he asked me what it was. So I said, 'Yes, it's from Dennis.' And then he told me how naughty that was and how I should never have got that letter and that I was not allowed to write back to him. I felt really upset that they had read the letter but most of all that I couldn't write to Dennis or see him at all. Then the head told me that Dennis would be banned from visiting the school for sixteen months. And that's what happened. We didn't see or write to each other for all that time.

Disabled people who grew up outside institutions enjoyed a little more freedom to form relationships with the opposite sex. But they too were confronted by prejudice and narrow attitudes which reinforced in them the feeling that they were outsiders. Many arrived at early adolescence with a negative image of themselves as a result of rejection at home, at school and at play. The sexual play widely indulged in at this age often brought more pain and rejection. David Swift was an adolescent in Nottingham in the 1940s who because of a muscular impairment walked with a limp.

We used to play a game when we were kids called 'True, Dare Kiss or Promise'. Now if you didn't do the dare you had to promise to do something else. So when it came to my turn they used to say to the girls, 'I dare you to kiss David Swift.' But they'd sooner do something else than kiss me. Because I think they were frightened of catching something from me. I couldn't understand it. You know, I'd got decent lips, you know what I mean. I used to feel so hurt and so left out, so hurtful. Such a hurtful game really when you think about it.

Feelings of anxiety and self-doubt became more intense when boys and girls began to experience a strong physical attraction for each other – often beginning in their early teens. Louis Goldberg moved to Brighton with his family at the age of five in 1921. He had cerebral palsy.

Because we lived at Brighton most of the Summer me and me mates used to go down the beach. But as I got into me teens I got so conscious of my body that I never wanted to take my clothes off to swim or sunbathe. I used to sit on the sands like a hunted animal. I had the feeling of wanting to hide myself away, not wanting any of my mates or any of the young girls hanging around to see how I looked different to them. Disability was always meant to be ugly and twisted and that's how I felt. So I'd stay all wrapped up in me clothes even in the hottest Summer. Those teenage years were a torment to me. Trying to fit in, trying to look like everyone else but always someone pointing out that I was different. Wanting desperately to take a girl out like the rest of the lads but I never had the courage to ask a girl. I never thought anyone would want to be seen with me.

Two of the main meeting places where teenagers met and formed relation-ships with the opposite sex in the first half of the century were the cinema and the dance hall. These places were designed solely for the able-bodied and were fraught with difficulties and anxieties for disabled young people. John Hughes was born in 1935 in Newcastle. He remembers how, on his first date, he tried to cover up the fact that he limped badly.

The first time I went to the picture house it turned out to be a real killer. There was a huge staircase that met in the middle. 'Course in all my excitement at having the girl agree to meet me I hadn't thought how difficult it would be to get in there. I tried to walk up the stairs and to look as if it was no effort for me. But once we'd got up to where the seats were I had to dash into the toilets and I was as sick as a dog. I was in so much pain, pretending all that while that everything was OK. I just couldn't turn around and say that I was cripple could I? You couldn't do that then. Had to pretend that you was normal.

As a teenager in Tottenham in the 1930s and 1940s Marie Hagger often went to the cinema with young men she knew.

Sometimes we sat through a film for three hours or so. I'd come out and I couldn't tell you one word that the film was about. It was terribly

Marie Hagger pictured with her boyfriend (later to become her husband) in a novelty cinema postcard of the 1930s.

boring. It took you all your patience just to sit there. Funnily enough one or two of them didn't even seem to notice my deafness, they were so wrapped up telling me about their own life stories, and that they wanted to be an air pilot or go in the navy or whatever, that they didn't seem to notice. But then sometimes they would look at me and I could see that first sign of impatience on their face. And they would say, 'Are you deaf Marie?' Because I wouldn't be answering their questions or something. I came out and I wouldn't be able to talk about the film at all and that meant goodbye because I always had a terrible fear inside me that once a boyfriend discovered how badly affected I was he wouldn't want to know anymore.

Similarly for David Swift the most difficult and embarrassing time was when the film was over.

I used to go to the Forum Picture House. And it was in the pictures that all the boys used to pick up girls. You could chat up a girl in the row in front of you and ask if you could take her home. She'd probably look around to see if you were nice enough. But the problem for me was walking home. What was I going to say to them? I couldn't say that I was born like this, that I had a disease or anything like that 'cos they wouldn't have had anything to do with me. So the minute I stepped onto the pavement outside the picture house, I took one step and they'd say, 'What you done to your leg? Why do you walk like that?' And then I'd tell all these different tales. I used to say all kinds of things. I'd done it playing football, fell out of a tree, jumped off a lorry or fell off a bus. It's got to be something that I'd done that was heroic.

To avoid rejection because of their disability some withdrew from social activities like cinema going where they might have developed relationships. Valerie Carr was born in 1935 in Southport and developed severe problems in walking as a result of a disability in her legs.

Certainly my disability inhibited my adolescent years. I remember a young man whom I liked very much asking me to go to the cinema but I declined because there were steps and I would need to ask for help to climb them. I was terrified he would think I was using this as an excuse to hold his hand and would be put off. So I didn't have boyfriends at all.

In dance halls young disabled people often felt even more vulnerable to ridicule and rejection. Much of what went on in dance halls was a ritual parade of masculinity and femininity by the able-bodied in order to attract the opposite sex. In this rather hostile setting young disabled people sometimes experienced total humiliation. In the 1930s Marjorie Jacques lived with her parents and sister in Sheerness in Kent.

Marjorie Jacques pictured in 1937 at the age of seventeen. Most disabled young people experienced isolation and rejection at this time.

My sister used to go off to dances and of course I was left at home. I used to love helping her get ready in all her glad rags. But naturally it made me feel left out, as if I wasn't being allowed to grow up and experience all the things that girls my age do. I was left sitting at home with my mother. I remember for a long time I had a crush on a young policeman that used to go around our way. Well, I was mad about him. I think he must have known it by the way I used to look at him. He used to chat to me sometimes when I was outside with my friends. Well, one day, I thought my dreams had come true because he asked me if I would go to his works dance with him. I felt so nervous for all the time up to the dance. What to wear and all that. He turned up for me and off we went to the dance. He sat me down at the edge so that I could watch all the couples dancing around and then he was off. Came back once with an ice-cream for me but other than that I didn't see him all night. I was heartbroken, to realise that he'd only asked me out of pity. And when I got home my mum said, 'Well, what did you expect? He wouldn't want to be seen taking you out.' I thought I'd never get over that.

To avoid this kind of pain many developed strategies to draw attention away from their disability. David Swift developed a strong sense of humour and acted the fool.

I wanted to dance. That was the only way that you could get a girl in your arms. You couldn't just grab one in the street could you? You'd got to figure out how to dance. So my sister learned me how to dance. She gets the four footsteps of Victor Silvester and paints them on the floor, right. And there I am walking on these footsteps with my sister.

David Swift (second from the right) pictured with his Teddy Boy friends in the early 1950s. To avoid the pain of rejection he developed a strong sense of humour and acted the fool.

And I goes to the dance hall and tries it and it turns out I'm doing the girl's part. She took the boy. But at least for the first time in my life I'd got my arms round a person of the opposite sex. And that's all I wanted. I didn't have many proper girlfriends, more casual acquaintances. Once they got to know the way I walked . . . I mean there were plenty of songs coming out then where they say, '*Look at the way she walks*'. Everything was '*He walks like an angel . . . Just walking in the rain . . . Walking my baby back home*'. And I'm thinking to myself about all these songs related to walking. And I couldn't even walk properly. What had I got to show? But I found the key pretty early. I found the key to getting a girl was to play the fool. I'd got to get their eyes away from my legs. So as long as I could keep them laughing I was all right. But as soon as I saw the eyes lowering I knew the danger was coming.

Marie Hagger avoided social situations in the dance hall where her deafness would be exposed by dancing practically all the time. Dancing was of great expressive importance to her.

I loved dance halls so much because no one spoke or if they did they were shouting – that was fine by me. The loudness of the music, the constant chatter of all the voices around me, meant one thing – it didn't matter if you were stone-deaf because no one was hearing anyway, everyone's mouthing to each other. I had the rhythm and the timing for dancing. I had all kinds of partners and none of them ever suspected that I was deaf. I could hear the loud music then, not what the tunes were so much as the beat. All those old numbers, they just send everybody wild and they were loud. There was no mistake, the floor actually moved. You could feel the vibrations. I was in my element; I loved it. I only had to wait for someone else to go onto the floor first before I knew what to do. Or I would ask someone, 'Is this a cha-cha, is it the waltz or is it a foxtrot or what?' The rest just fell into a pattern, it was easy. I could be myself. I could dance how I wanted to dance and I felt freedom. I felt all the pent up emotions come out of me when I was dancing. It was purely self-expression and that gave me tremendous satisfaction simply because I was doing something I really liked. I met several boys dancing. They wanted to go somewhere to sit down and converse and I knew that that was very often all they wanted to do. A few dances and right, sit down and have a talk. And somehow I had to sort of swerve them away from that and back into dancing because as soon as I found myself alone with them all the old fears came flying back to me. I couldn't take it.

David Swift singing at Butlin's in the mid-'50s. To overcome his feelings of inferiority he became a singer with a rock and roll band.

Albert Brown was brought up in Salford in the 1920s. To overcome his feelings of inferiority on the dance floor he became a musician in a dance band.

Because of my surgical boot I couldn't dance. And that's what you had to do to meet a girl in those days. I'd go to the dance halls with me mates and sit around not wanting to get up and have a go for fear of making a fool of meself. Sometimes I'd get chatting to a girl and pluck up the courage to ask her to the pictures or somewhere, 'cause that was the other great courting place at the time. But more than likely she'd turn me down flat. All through me teens I had rejection after rejection from lasses. Every time it was always a blow. It made you feel so conscious of the way you looked and how you walked. I remember that I used to wonder whether there would ever be a girl who would go out with me. Anyway after a few years I'd had enough. I decided to get rid of me boot. It was more difficult for me to walk then but at least I had more confidence in meself. I didn't feel as if I stuck out so much like a sore thumb. And about that time I got into playing the drums. That really gave me something to hide behind. I played at lots of dance halls. It was my way of getting accepted without having to go through all the humiliation of not being able to dance or sitting on the edge of things.

Despite attempts like these by young disabled people to avoid prejudice and to win social acceptance their overwhelming experience in relationships with the opposite sex was one of rejection. Even if they succeeded in forming such a relationship it would often be ended by parents who did not want their able-bodied son or daughter to go out with a disabled person. John Hughes:

Parents were always a stumbling block. If I ever managed to get a girl and took her out more than a couple of times then it was home to meet the parents for tea. The look on their faces said it all. 'You're not going out with him again. A cripple!' I always wanted them to know what I was really, that my legs didn't make any difference. But I knew what they were thinking. They didn't want a disabled person in the family, married to their daughter. What would their grandchildren turn out like? And sure enough I wouldn't see the girl again.   Marie Hagger:

If a boy ever mentioned taking me home to his parents that would be the end. I knew straight away that my defences would be down. His mother would see through me, expose me. I went to one boy's parents once and the very next day he called it off with me. Even though they hadn't said so to me, I knew that they had told him to finish with me because they didn't want a deaf woman in the family. And that was another rejection. So if ever a relationship got as far as that level, 'Come home and have tea', that's when I opted out.

CHAPTER FIVE
SHATTERED DREAMS

In 1933 eighteen year old Ted Williams set out from Sheffield on a protest march to London, organised by the National League of the Blind. The aim was to bring attention to the unemployment, low wages and poor working conditions that blind people had to endure.

> There was more or less a national uprising. The whole of England and the whole of Scotland decided to have a march to London. The Scots came down marching all the way and picking up the English blind as they went. They arrived in Sheffield and all our workshop joined them and we marched down to London. I was jiggered, it seemed such a long walk to me, like it did to a lot of us. Salvation Army Halls we slept there, they took care of us for a night. And the people in the towns and villages they were very, very good and they used to troop out and bring up soup and sandwiches. Actually I am certain I got more on that march than I

Mass demonstrations of blind workers – and sighted sympathisers in Trafalgar Square in 1920. Blind workers marched to London from all over Britain to protest against low wages and poor working conditions in 1920, 1933 and 1947.

Demonstrations of blind workers in London in 1836. Blind people – organised by the National League of the Blind – were the most militant of all disabled groups before the last war.

got for a month at home. And every morning we pushed on a few more miles until we eventually got to London. We stood in Trafalgar Square and shouted for what improvements we wanted. We sent a deputation of shop stewards into Parliament and I might add they got nowhere at all but it at least awakened people to our conditions.

Before the last war disabled people formed an underclass neglected by society and denied opportunities in the world of work. The training they received in the institutions where they grew up – and the workshops attached to them – prepared them for a lowly role in society. They were trained to enter into a very narrow range of occupations. Girls were generally taught dressmaking, embroidery, laundry work or domestic service. As 'apprentices' they were often paid nothing for their labour or at most 'pocket money', even though institutions and workshops often sold their wares for profit. Mary Baker began her occupational training at Halliwick Home for Crippled Girls at the age of sixteen in 1938.

When I finished schooling, I had to do my needlework training. It was either needlework or domestic science. Well, I wasn't keen on domestic science, so I said I'd do needlework. So Matron said it would take two years. We had to wear all these serge clothes, the same as we wore when we were girls and we got all the same discipline. The needlework we did started off very plain. We had all the stitching to do, then we had to do buttonholes of all description and if we passed all that we could go onto something more elaborate. It was mostly underclothes that we made. Beautiful silk stuff, and we used to do scallops on them and this lace work. Satin nightdresses and pants and camiknickers. I don't know where they went but I think they were done for orders and some went up to shops in London. We weren't paid anything even though the goods all went out perfect. And I always used to wish that I could wear some of those clothes that we made. We'd never had silk or anything next to our bodies, we had no idea. But we used to put the things up to our faces and feel it. Such a beautiful feeling. But we still had to wear our awful, hard uniforms and never saw any of the stuff we made once it was finished. It sort of gave you an inferiority complex, because what else could we do? We were taught needlework and nothing else, this was what our life would have to be. And I thought, 'My word, is that all I'm going to do all my life?' This was all disabled people were allowed to do, we weren't allowed to put our minds to anything else, because they thought we weren't fit to do it.

Boys were often taught tailoring, carpentry, basketmaking matmaking or bootmaking and repairing. Ernest Williams was an inmate of the Birmingham Blind Institution in the 1920s.

At the end of my educational life at sixteen, I simply the next day went into the workshops. It had been decided that I would go for boot and shoe making and repairing. I was to be trained then sent back to the little village where I had come from, there to have a wooden shed adjacent to my cottage home which would be my workshop. And so it was. It was a very slow and sort of tortuous training. One first learnt to sandpaper things, that sort of thing and then to put a heel on a shoe and finish it off. That might take you half a term. And the system allowed for three years to become qualified to decently sole and heel a pair of shoes. Much of the training was pure repetition and not by any means progressive. Not uncommon to take weeks over a simple task. People ask me whether I wasn't bored to death. But the truth of the matter is that we were psychologically adapted to the acceptance of one's lot. And the lot was that you were in a craft and it was the best way you could

(Overleaf) *Girls basketmaking at an 'institution for the blind' in the 1900s. Disabled people were trained to enter a very narrow range of occupations.*

earn yourself a living. When we started our training we didn't get any pocket money at all. But at a point in our training when we were considered to be a productive unit, in other words the work you did didn't have to be stripped down and done again, then you got a very small amount listed against your name so that at the end of the term you could pick it up, say five shillings. I always had notions that I could do much better and of course it was always a constant source of regret to me that I went into handicrafts. It was a frustrating business. I used to be at the bench mending a pair of shoes and I used to daydream of doing something else, something outstanding in another field, or using one's brain.

Ted Williams left the Manchester Road Royal Institution for the Blind in Sheffield at the age of sixteen in 1931. He was immediately transferred to the nearby Sharrow Lane workshops.

On the day that I left school I was told that I would be going into the mat shop and that was that. There was no choice at all. We had twenty odd looms in our mat shop at the workshops, big thundering great things they were. And the common run of the mat maker was that you stood winding yarn round a steel rod and thumping the big heavy baton down to bang the rows up together. We did that then hour after hour, year after year, lifetime after lifetime. You either did that particular trade you were put to when you left school or you did nothing at all. As it happens I was fairly capable at mat making but I hated the job. And the money we had especially on apprentice rate was very poor. I started with four shillings a week and if I wore me socks out because we'd got to keep the two pedals on the loom going with our feet all the time and so our socks wore out pretty quick then I had to buy me own socks out of that. I took bread and dripping for my dinner because there was no way of affording anything more.

These workshops – most of which were run by charities or by local councils – paid a small weekly wage to disabled workers who had completed their 'apprenticeships'. But they enjoyed little freedom or independence. There were elaborate rules and regulations governing their behaviour and they had few rights at work. Often they were treated like children. This patronising treatment was especially upsetting to adult disabled workers who sometimes had little choice but to spend their whole working lives in these workshops. Ted Williams:

There were instances like when the superintendent of our workshop would say, 'Teddy, what are you doing here Teddy?' And I'd be a grown man in my thirties. It was always a patronising tone. I once remember that I was stood out on the veranda, I'd gone out for a breather because it was a boiling hot day and the mat shop roof was made of glass. And the overseer came out and patted me on the shoulder and said, 'Get inside Teddy.' And I was supposed to go all red in the face and run back in the greenhouse and that's how it went with most of them. Even if we went to the toilet and we were above what the foreman thought the time limit he'd come in and say, 'Have you finished that job yet Ted? You'll not finish it there will you?' And so we always felt that we had to run out and get on with the job. We were governed by rules much as we were when we were at the blind school. As a result we had a signalling system. And that was that if a sighted person in authority walked into the department then a partially-sighted worker who saw him would shout 'Bodkin'. That meant there was a stranger in the camp and to watch what you were up to, be a bit careful with your comments. If you were telling a sexy joke that would end immediately. But even with the system there were a few unfortunate incidents. I myself got into serious trouble one time at least. I didn't hear the signal and I happened to be saying something quite uncomplimentary about the superintendent. So of course she heard me and I got suspended for a week without pay.

The sheltered workshops only provided jobs for a relatively small minority of disabled people. In the early part of the century there were places for around 15,000 men and women in these workshops. In some areas there were virtually no sheltered workshops at all for disabled people to attend. For example in the East End of London on the eve of the First World War there were 650 blind inhabitants but no workshops for them. In London as a whole at this time there were around 3,500 blind people but there was workshops provision for just 250.

Most had to try to find jobs in a labour market that was geared exclusively to the needs of the able-bodied. There was generally no concern with providing access or facilities that would enable disabled people to work in offices or factories. They were generally best provided for if they came from a family which had its own business. Many family businesses made an effort to cater for the special needs of a disabled member of the family. Louis Goldberg left school in Brighton when he was sixteen in 1932. His father ran a motor business next to the family home.

My father had a garage for motor car repairs and engineering. I used to hang around the place watching the men work on the cars and learn how they did everything. Anyhow when I left school it was a question of what I could do for work. I wasn't fixed very well for walking and getting about. One day we were in the garage and my father struck on the idea of building me a kind of sliding cart which I could lie down on and shift myself about on under the cars. And that's how I started working as a mechanic. I could do everything once I was on that cart and from having grown up all around cars I picked it all up quick enough.

Louis Goldberg pictured in 1936, aged twenty, working as a mechanic in his father's motor business. His father built him a sliding cart so that he could get underneath the cars to repair them.

That was the first step to me learning to drive myself and really a whole world opened up to me around cars and work. I adapted a car so that I could drive it on my own. There wasn't much I didn't know about cars in those days. I certainly don't know where I would have ended up if I hadn't had the chance to work with my father and my brothers. I wouldn't have fancied being shut up in some factory or other or just stuck at home all day long. I wanted to get my hands dirty and to learn a proper trade. I was just lucky enough to be able to do that.

Some employers offered jobs to disabled workers, often giving the impression that this was a charitable and paternalistic gesture. But beneath the surface there was usually an exploitative intention; disabled workers were normally only paid around half to two thirds of the rates paid to the able-bodied. Most employers however simply rejected disabled workers out of hand. As a result looking for a job could be a demoralising experience. Ron Moore, born in Finsbury, North London, 1923, lost both his legs after he was run over by a bus at the age of ten. He began looking for work in the late 1930s.

They didn't give me any special training at the school for crippled boys where I went and I had no qualifications. Roehampton delivered one pair of artificial legs to me, there was no advice, no help, just the usual 'good luck mate'. There was no help from the labour exchange either. It was down to me to get a job. Well, I desperately wanted to work, I wanted an office job, to be a clerk. I wrote to some offices in the City but they didn't reply or they rejected me out of hand. So I decided to go door-to-door looking for a job. For six months I went day after day to banks and insurance offices in the City. I dressed up very smartly in a suit. Sometimes I managed to get to see the manager but I wasn't in very good shape by the time I got to the interview. The artificial legs rubbed blisters where they joined the tops of my legs and they often bled. It was very painful walking around so when I got to the manager's office I had to ask to sit down. That didn't make a very good impression because in those days you were expected to stand to attention, cap in hand. Well, they always said the same thing, 'You've got no legs have you, I'm afraid we can't employ you.' After a bit I used to get very angry and I'd start arguing and telling them what I thought of them. But it didn't make any difference. I was very upset. It was hell.

Ron Moore, aged 16, in his best suit. In the late 1930s he was rejected by countless banks and insurance companies because of his disability – he had artificial legs.

Deep-seated prejudice and the narrow attitudes of employers led to a very high level of unemployment amongst disabled people. In the 1920s almost half of all adults who were deaf were unemployed, despite the efforts of deaf missioners – churchmen attached to institutions for deaf people who tried to find them jobs. Unemployment however was highest amongst blind people. At the turn of the century out of a total blind population of around 35,000 in Britain, the majority were unemployed with more than 5,000 receiving Poor Law parish relief. In the Depression years of the 1930s unemployment amongst blind people rose even more. In 1936 about 35,000 out of a total blind population of 40,000 were unemployed. Most were classified as unemployable by labour exchanges. In addition to those disabled from birth there was also very high unemployment around this time amongst disabled war veterans and men and women disabled by accidents. 40,000 men had lost limbs in the First World War and during the inter-war years many of these had no jobs and were dependent on inadequate pensions and charity handouts. Similarly men and women who lost limbs at work usually received little or no compensation and they too often found themselves on the bread line.

Unemployment brought absolute poverty for many disabled people. Dependent on parish relief for their survival, many gravitated to the poorest, cheapest slum streets in the big cities. Here there was often a concentration of disabled men and women living in rented tenement blocks or cheap lodging houses. Campbell Road in North Islington – regarded in the 1920s and 1930s as the 'worst street in North London' – was one such street where disabled people congregated. Here the poverty was so extreme that in the winter some front doors were chopped up by the residents for firewood and on hot summer nights hundreds would sleep out on the streets to avoid infestation from plagues of bugs which thrived in their squalid homes. The street's inhabitants – whose lives are documented in detail in Jerry White's *The Worst Street in London: Campbell Bunk Between the Wars* (1986) – eked out a living through begging, petty crime and occasional part-time work. Amongst them were Mr Drover a one-legged jobbing signwriter who lost a leg below the knee though an abscess at the age of eleven; Henry Gough, a 'deaf-mute' of no occupation who was convicted of stealing a fellow lodger's boots at the Campbell Road Lodging House 'So that he might have a better chance of getting work'; blind Mr Chine who stood outside Finsbury Park station selling matches; George Thomas, a disabled coal miner who was convicted of peddling without a licence; Reginald Inksipp, blinded by a bayonet would made extra money as an organ grinder; and James Leary, a 'persistent beggar' who had received a gunshot wound during the First World War and was unable to work.

Len Tasker who had polio entered a similar world of poverty and deprivation in Coventry when he left hospital at the age of nineteen in 1934.

Selling matches in London around the turn of the century. Unemployment was highest amongst blind people. They were often forced to resort to begging and street hawking in order to survive.

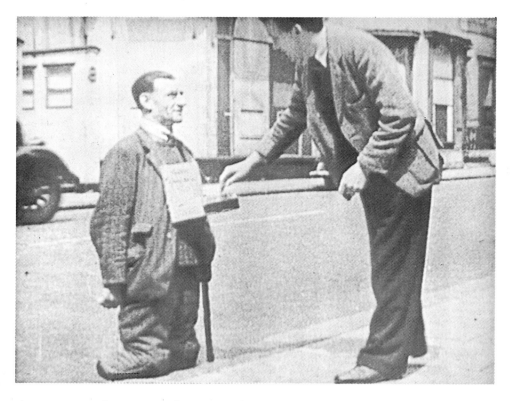

A war veteran begging on the streets of London in the 1930s. 39,000 men lost their limbs during the First World War and many were dependent on inadequate pensions and charity handouts.

When I first came out of hospital I thought it would be all rosy and that my life would get started then. But all I saw was poverty all around. Lots of disabled men begging in the streets, selling reels of cotton and matches and things like that. It was the thirties and there were no chances for the disabled then. I was totally dependent on my brother and his wife for money and food. There was nobody who would give me a job. I couldn't get any social benefits because I didn't have any insurance stamps because I had never worked with being in hospital. You had to be working twelve months before you could get means tested for unemployment benefit so I was caught in a hole. If it hadn't have been for my brother working then I would have been on the streets. As it was there was never enough to go round the three of us. I felt so useless but I couldn't get a job. I'd never been trained for anything. I did a bit of handicrafts, making duchess sets for the neighbours and getting orders from them for a bit of pocket money. In the end I got a job peeling potatoes in the local fish and chip shop. I was so pleased to get a few pennies even though it was such long hours and boring work. I had to keep it a secret from my brother, what I was doing. He would have been angry if he'd have found out exactly what my job was. But I was so desperate for the insurance stamps that I would have done absolutely anything.

Short time working in the sheltered workshops during the depression years of the 1930s meant that some of their workers who had little or no family support also became virtually destitute. Ted Williams:

We was on three days a month at the workshop at that time. Well now the other months we got domiciliary so called. That was no more than twelve or fifteen shillings and you had to pay everything out of that and live off that. The favourite was to give food tickets, not money. I myself used to go down to the Board of Guardians Relief place at the bottom of our street and they would give me some of these tickets and with those I would go and get my week's groceries at a certain shop. And we were given the bare minimum to pay the rent as well. One of the chief things that the blind had to do was to go around pubs and almost any other place and play the piano accordion. In fact most of our workers at Sharrow Lane workshops were dependent on a pub job on the weekend as well as the work at Sharrow just to get by. I myself for quite a few years used to go round mostly on a Saturday night generally where there was a pub where there were plenty of people in and I would sit there desperately hoping that someone would ask me to strike up a tune on my accordion. More often than not someone would. And then I would go round with the hat. If I struck lucky I would get quite a few shillings. And believe you me it made all the difference in the world. It was terribly hard. Well, it's bound to affect you. I myself have gone more than once, many times in fact, from Saturday to Wednesday without a thing to eat. The worst was when you came to go to bed hungry. I would lie in bed and think of all sorts of things just to keep my mind off the fact that my stomach was whittling. I'd be in agony with this gnawing feeling in my stomach. It really boiled down to either you bought food or you paid your rent. And that's what it was like. I once remember that I just had nowhere to go at all, and it was belting it down with rain. I was walking down the main street in Sheffield and I was just crying to myself. What could I do? Where could I go? That particular time I sat most of the night on a seat in Endcliffe Woods. I sat on that form and I said to myself, 'Don't be daft, men don't cry.' Which of course I did. I'll admit I did.

The coming of the Second World War in 1939 was to transform radically the working lives of disabled people in Britain. As the able-bodied were called up into the armed forces there was a desperate need for workers on the Home Front. This labour shortage was solved by the recruitment of women and disabled people to work in essential services, hospitals, factories, offices and on farms. The story of women's war work is comparatively well-documented but the important role played by disabled people on the Home Front has been largely ignored. Their recruitment and – in some cases – their rapid promotion to positions of responsibility began in an ad hoc and informal way. Management suddenly realised the hidden potential of disabled workers who

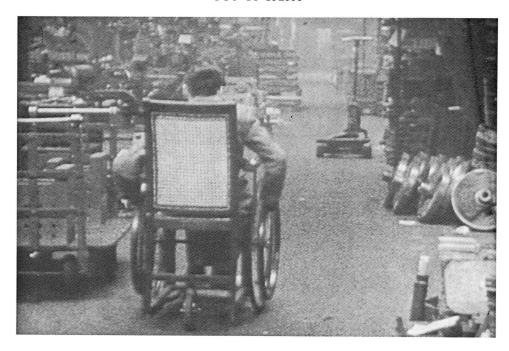

A disabled worker makes his way to his machine in a munitions factory near Portsmouth during the Second World War. Disabled people played an important role on the Home Front during the war.

until then had invariably only been considered for the most menial jobs and paid the lowest wages. At the outset of the war Ernest Williams was working in a typing pool in Hereford – he had re-trained from being a bootmaker to a shorthand typist to increase his chances of getting work.

> When the war came a lot of the young men with responsibility went off and joined the forces and so the firm became rather short of trained staff. I had always been the dogsbody really, shorthand typing all day. That went on I suppose until the effect of the absence of the men got through to the management. One morning the chief accountant called me in and said to me, 'You've been with us a fair time now haven't you Williams? You know this business fairly well.' I said 'Yes sir'. 'The only trouble with you is that you can't bloody well see.' Anyway he suggested promoting me to be in charge of one of the departments and getting me a secretary type person to help me with my correspondence and such like. She was a girl, I think her name was Nicholson, copper coloured hair, lovely girl. And she used to fetch things for me, get files, read difficult handwriting and so on. She acted as a pair of eyes for me really and it worked out very well. They doubled my wages inside a week. But more important of course I was doing something which depended on my ability to do it. And I thought I'd arrived.

Some of those disabled people who had been unemployed or subsisting on part-time work for several years before the war now at last found permanent jobs – sometimes with the possibility of promotion. Len Tasker:

I tried for a job at a factory. I went up there, so pleased at the thought that I would be doing some proper work for myself as well as for the war effort. Anyway they gave me the job. I was rate-fixing clerk in this big factory and well, I never looked back from there on. The war certainly opened up doors for me as a disabled person. I think it opened up opportunities for people with disabilities generally. I would never have been given the chance to do that job if it hadn't have been for them looking for extra workers in the war but as it happened I did really well in the job and got promoted.

There were new opportunities for women too. In 1942 Mary Baker became a nurse at Halliwick Home for Crippled Girls where she had grown up.

Before the war no nurse was allowed to go in if you were disabled. But as the war was on, nurses were short, they'd gone off to war. They just had to put up with whatever we had. So I asked the Matron if I could do children's nursing and she said that as the war was on she would give me a chance. So I started off nursing. I don't think that I would have been given the chance if the war had not been on. There was two of us at Halliwick who were nurses then. I had my bad leg and the other girl only had one arm and we managed quite well. I was determined to do something with my life. I loved looking after the little children. Lots of them had callipers and things like that. Some of the nurses were a bit rough. They said that the children couldn't feel anything in

Mary Baker pictured in her nurse's uniform at Halliwick Home for Crippled Girls. The war opened up many new opportunities for disabled women.

their legs so it didn't matter how we treated them. But I felt that I understood them more because of what I'd been through when I was a child. I felt that they did have feelings and I used to be very kind and put them into the plasters and wrap the bandages round and put them back to bed. And if they were uncomfortable I used to go back and say, are you all right and I did them all up again. I had a lot of patience with the children and I used to sit and talk to them when they'd gone to bed and see if they could go off to sleep, read little books to them. We had one or two very small children who were homesick so you just cuddled them and loved them and you did what you could for them. You weren't allowed to get too intimate with them, because it was wrong, matron wouldn't allow that. But we used to do things that matron never knew anything about so this is how we carried on. I really enjoyed the work and my legs didn't interfere with what I did, I made sure of that, because otherwise matron wouldn't have kept me on with everything. And the other senior nurses were very good to me because they helped me when I stumbled over anything that I just couldn't do, such as lifting the mattress over or lifting girls, they used to come along and help you. Being a nurse, it gave me a lot of pride especially when I got my uniform and I looked so smart because I thought I'd never be able to do anything in life.

By 1941 the need for labour was so urgent that Ernest Bevin the Minister of Labour initiated a plan to recruit disabled people en masse into the workforce. In the next four years 426,000 disabled men and women – many of whom had been officially classified as 'unemployable' at labour exchanges – were interviewed by Ministry of Labour officers to assist them in finding jobs. Of these 310,806 were placed in employment or were given training which enabled them to get jobs. In May 1941 Ron Moore was sent to a training college in Leatherhead and was then given assistance in finding a job.

The labour exchange sent me to train for technical drawing office work. It was all very exciting and the Canadian Army was stationed nearby. We helped them draw and design a mechanism on their twenty-five pounder guns. They used to be operated by a cord nut and we developed a foot operated lever so that a man could sit behind the gun all the time. Then it was made in the workshop.

When I finished my training the labour exhange tried to get me a job and I went around to different places with a national service officer to see the bosses about taking me on. I got two or three rejections then they took me at an electrical factory in St. Mary Cray in Kent. They made electrical motors for the armed forces. My job was to be junior draughtsman in the drawing office. It was very hard, the hours were long. And because there was no accommodation in the town we all had to sleep in temporary huts in the car park next to the factory. Well they were testing engines all night which kept us awake. But it was very exciting being part of the design team. The other men accepted me and helped me, I was a sort of novelty, a lad with no legs, some of them couldn't believe it. But we were all doing our bit for the war effort and that drew us together.

Labour exchanges however were more vigorous in their attempts to find jobs for disabled men rather than disabled women. As a result disabled women often had to wait longer to be placed in employment. Jenny Waller was born in 1920 with cerebral palsy in Burneside, in the Lake District. Although looking for work for several years, she was only found a job in the later stages of the war.

I can remember reading a headline in the newspaper one Sunday, 'CRIPPLES CAN DO VITAL WAR WORK'. It seemed as though this would be the chance I'd been waiting for to work. So I sent off a letter straight away. The reply came back that it was for men only, they'd not thought of women. I was always typing letters off for jobs. Endless letters asking for employment but receiving the same disappointing replies. I had testimonials to show my ability but these didn't alter one iota the fact of my handicap. It seemed they didn't really have any use for me. My hopes rose with each new application and fell with each new rejection. I wrote to labour exchanges all over the country! Anyway, finally, quite unexpectedly, I got a visitor from my local labour exchange. She told me that they'd got a job at a Royal Ordnance factory in Swynnerton near Stafford. All the amenities were on site, I would live in a hostel and work for the catering manager as his canteen storekeeping clerk. My heart missed a beat, I was absolutely delighted. It was another step forwards to independence. I was self-supporting at last and I had a well-paid, satisfying job to my credit. For the first time in my life I could start to save something for a rainy day and spend my own money as I pleased. It was a wonderful feeling and I revelled in being my own mistress at last.

Disabled people were integrated into the workplace, working alongside the able-bodied. In some factories the hearing learned sign language to communicate with deaf workers. And more and more disabled people were given skilled and responsible jobs. In all around half a million disabled people were recruited into full-time employment during the war. To aid this recruitment drive the government produced many training films presenting a positive image of disability. And newsreel companies ran items celebrating the everyday working lives of disabled people. It was all part of a new recognition of their economic importance at a time when their labour power was desperately needed.

Signing in a munitions factory during the last war. In some factories the hearing learned sign language to communicate with deaf workers.

When the war was over it appeared that many of the gains made by disabled people during the war would be consolidated and extended. The Disabled Persons Act of 1944 gave the state the power to force employers to take a prescribed quota of disabled workers. The Labour government elected the following year was committed to the creation of a welfare state and to greater opportunities for disadvantaged groups. Films of the time produced by the Central Office of Information like *Back To Normal* (1945) gave an optimistic view of the future for disabled people. *Back To Normal* was presented by a worker who had lost his arm in the war. He and other disabled people are seen getting jobs and working alongside the able bodied in factories. He describes to camera, how lingering patronising attitudes to disabled people must be overcome.

'A lot of people, well-meaning people too, think that if you've only one arm they've got to get you an easy job like a clerk or a lift attendant. At

(Opposite) *Images from the 1942 Pathe newsreel* Blind Farmer Carries On. *The film celebrated the work of 'Blind John' who could do all the jobs on the farm, including delivering the milk to his local community in Northumberland. Many newsreels and training films made during the war years promoted a positive image of disability. It was all part of a new recognition of their economic importance at a time when their labour power was desperately needed.*

BLIND FARMER CARRIES ON

An image from the government training film Back to Normal, *made in 1945. It was one of many films made in the immediate post war years which gave a very optimistic view of the future for disabled people.*

first I thought they were right. But if you've been an engineer – what's wrong with the same job? I find I can manage pretty well and it's a simple matter for a government training centre to give you the correct tools.'

But although the Labour government made some efforts to integrate those disabled by the war back into the workforce – principally through government training centres – there was little or no support for those disabled from birth. Now that the urgent wartime need for their labour had gone many were demoted or discarded by employers on a mass scale – as were women – to be replaced by able-bodied men returning from the armed services to their civilian jobs. Disabled young people looking for their first job found it very difficult to find employment at this time. Gerald Turner was looking for work in the late 1940s when he was in his twenties. He had cerebral palsy.

I went to the Labour Exchange and they just used to throw me out and say there wasn't any work for somebody like me. They didn't think I was any use to anyone. I was desperate to get a job. It was so boring sitting around at home all day while my brothers and that went out to work. I would have done anything but they weren't interested one bit. So I thought that I would have to do something for myself. I asked people if they wanted their gardens done or their allotments turned over. I used to be quite good with a spade. It was tiring but at least I was doing something useful. I used to look after the veg for folk and dig it up and take it round to places. I still went to the Labour every week but they never had anything for me. So I just went on working really hard at the gardens. Someone would give me the odd copper now and then but mostly it was for nothing. It was hard to get by with no pocket money even and living with me mum and dad but I wanted to prove that I could do a job.

Disabled young people entering jobs in the late 1940s and early 1950s were often confronted with the same prejudices and narrow attitudes that had been so dominant before the war. David Swift began work at the Raleigh bicycle factory in Nottingham in 1951 at the age of fifteen.

The men got paid on the amount of frames they did and they got a target of making two thousand bicycle frames on an eight hour shift. Whatever they decided I had to keep up with them, and they gave me the jobs with the most walking. I must have walked miles every day. And the men would see the way I walked and it probably became acceptable, in their minds. But they never considered that I ought to have a job that was sitting down. Nobody ever considered that. The foreman gave me a bad time, he didn't like me. He used to jibe me and walk behind me, I could actually feel what he was doing. He was trying to make the men laugh and taking it out of me and shouting 'Hoppy'. They thought it were funny to shout 'Hopalong Cassidy'. You know, when I walked up to him he actually mocked the way I walked. That was his humour, but to me it was the most hurtful thing.

They treated me like crap anyway. I was there over two and a half years and at eighteen you were supposed to get full money but they never paid me full money. I didn't get my rise like the other men. They seemed to say that they were doing me a favour by having me working there. And yet I was working very hard. And the men knew this. Of course it was semi-skilled but I wasn't an apprentice anymore. I had become a sort of lynch pin. After that I had a falling out with the foreman, I told him what to do with his job and that I wanted the same money as everybody else. I swore at him and so he had me up to this office to see the manager. And to go in there was like going into the most holy of temples. And the manager says to me, 'Now you've got to behave yourself because if you don't you're going to get the sack and you're not going to find a job anywhere else.' But I said that I wasn't getting the same money as everybody else. He said, 'Look here, you're very fortunate to be working here, you being crippled like you are.' That was like a red rag to a bull, that was it to me. So a day later I went and put my notice in.

Insecurity at work and fear of unemployment led many to try to hide their disability as far as possible. Marie Hagger worked in a hairdressing salon after the war. She was very concerned to keep her deafness a secret from the staff and the customers.

When I went for the interview for the job the governor he did so much talking that quite frankly he didn't even notice I couldn't hear. Often I tried to lipread what the customers were saying which was acceptable once they were sitting in the chair with their heads straight up. But as soon as I started to wash their hair their head was down. Sometimes they were still talking and it was hopeless. I could feel at the back of their necks that they were talking, I could feel the vibration, but I had no idea what they were saying. And then I tried lipreading through the mirror. Not too bad. Except some hardly used their mouths at all. They spoke almost through clenched teeth. But the difficulties of trying to keep my deafness a secret to the shop staff, the customers, the clientele was traumatic. I felt that I was going to be exposed. And when that did happen I was going to be rejected. One day I got talking to the girls as we often did in the back of the shop. And I don't know what made me do it but I asked one of them what she earned. And when she told me I fell down. It was a lot more than I got but there was absolutely nothing I could do about it. What could I say? 'You are not paying me enough I am leaving'. Did I really think that I could leave and go somewhere else? The short answer to that was no I couldn't. I dreaded the sack. I dreaded thinking this deafness is going to give me the sack.

In the late 1940s and early 1950s disabled people were again increasingly pushed back into segrated workshops and factories of which the largest was the government supported Remploy group. This system of segregated labour operated in its most extreme form in mental handicap hospitals. Evelyn King, born in 1945, has spent all her life from the age of five onwards in a mental handicap hospital in the North of England.

The first thing they tried me on, the first day they put me on cards and envelopes. You know, to put them in piles, cards in one pile and envelopes in another then after a while when I'd been on that, she tried me on something like bun cases or cocktail sticks. In the old days, nobody got money in them days, years ago nobody got money in their hand and I knew what I would like to spend it on. I felt a bit awful when you had to work and didn't get paid as well. I would have liked to be rich in them days. I would have liked some nice clothes or to buy some nice perfume, soap and talc.

Some like Ted Williams tried to break the mould of segregated work in institutions and workshops by trying to form their own small business. Ted began a small independent workshop in Sheffield just after the war. But there was strong resistance from the blind establishment.

I'd always had ambitions to break away. I decided that I would give it a try and I started to save up some money from playing the piano accordion all around Sheffield, in the pubs and clubs and so on. And then when I had enough I opened a small shop and set up in my own right. Oh but I had terrific opposition from the workers themselves, and from the staff the sighted staff in the blind workshops. You see they regarded it as a kind of desertion. They didn't like people like me. They liked the steady, rock-like people that were just content to do the same thing year in, year out. I had the shop two years and then I sold it and applied to go back to my old job in the mat shop, and you wouldn't credit what a pantomime it was for me to get back. And when I got back I was put on lower class work, far underneath less capable fellows than myself. And they seemed to resent anyone trying to break away. The theory used to be once you got to the blind establishment and became a matmaker, basket maker or whatever you were there for life.

(Below and overleaf) *Women at work in mental handicap hospitals in the North of England in the 1950s. The system of segrated labour operated in its most extreme form in mental handicap hospitals.*

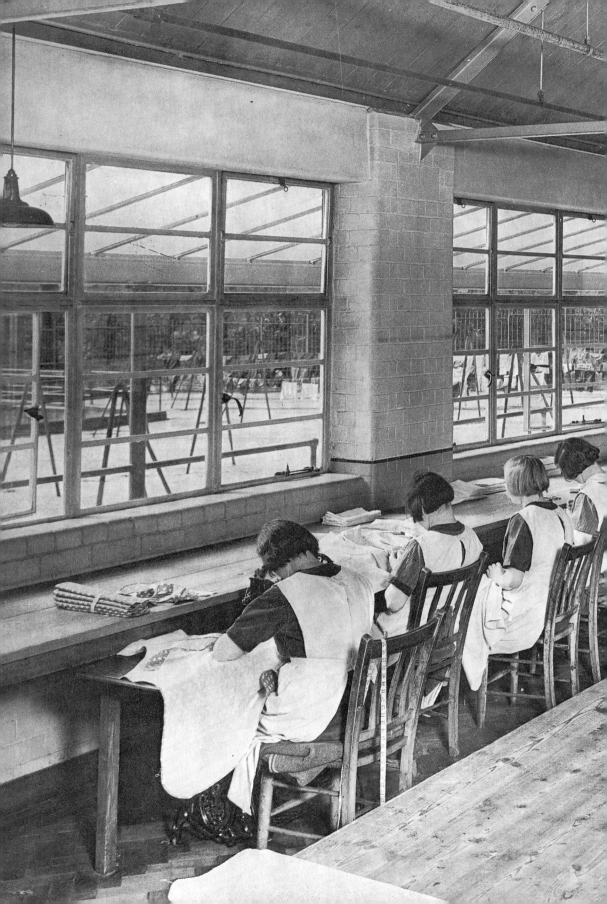

CHAPTER SIX

FORBIDDEN LOVE

When Mary Baker left Halliwick Home for Crippled Girls in North London in 1947 at the age of twenty-five she could not imagine that she might one day have a family of her own.

> I never dreamt that I'd get married and I certainly didn't think that I'd have children. It's something out of this world to me. Being disabled they made you feel as though you had no use in the world and so why become a mother. They didn't give you any help or encouragement that you needed to help you along that line. It made me feel I wasn't whole, it made me feel sort of not clean enough to have children so to speak. They made you feel small and that you weren't suitable to be a wife or mother.

Most disabled young people had very low expectations of ever finding a partner or of having children. The majority who had been brought up in institutions found any serious relationship with a member of the opposite sex very difficult. They often had a very low sense of self-esteem and felt very insecure about themselves and their bodies. Many withdrew from social situations. The most common reaction of a disabled young man or woman to an advance from a potential partner was rejection. At the heart of this reaction was a deep fear of any possible intimate or sexual contact. Consequently many disabled people brought up in institutions remained single and without a serious relationship long after they had left them. Mary Baker:

> Sex was never mentioned at Halliwick and when I left I had a weird feeling of something of the unknown which I didn't really want to get involved in. So when ever I met boys I just used to ignore them so to speak. Or if they came near me I just shooed them off. I felt that I didn't know enough, I'd never had any learning about things and I was frightened. I never let boys near me. If they ever started kissing me then that was the end of that friendship. I was frightened and this is all there was to it. I had no idea what boys meant really. They were the opposite sex and that was that. Maybe it was because I'd always mixed with girls that I was frightened. I just used to avoid boys getting near me, I wouldn't allow them to touch me. I'd sometimes make a date but I'd never turn up. So the poor boy would wait, I've seen them waiting for me. I lost my nerve at the last minute and I'm sure it's because matron would never let us have anything to do with anyone of the opposite sex at Halliwick.

The few who did form romantic and sexual relationships soon after leaving institutions often fell victim to the naivety and ignorance about members of the opposite sex derived from their rigid institutional upbringing. Sometimes this led to hasty and disastrous marriages. Ted Williams left the Royal Manchester Road Institution for the Blind at the age of sixteen in 1931. He married a sighted young woman soon afterwards.

> You see when we left school in that condition we were no judge of a woman, of a girl, we'd no judgement. Now I went to this particular house and heard this girl speak and she, she'd just come from Hull, she'd got a kind of accent and to me it were terrific. I fell immediately for that girl and the upshot of it was that for some reason or other, she was fully sighted incidentally, for some reason or other she did like me. So the upshot was that we got married very quickly. I met her in January and we got married in the first week in April and well, I regretted it because things turned out terrible. But part of that was due to the fact that owing to my cloistered upbringing up at the Blind School I'd just no judgement of a woman. All I knew was that I heard her voice, I liked her, I loved her, that's what I thought and I married her as quickly as possible. She wasn't eighteen, she was just seventeen and I claim that if I'd had a less cloistorous bringing up with women, the opposite sex, I'd have a better judgement. I wouldn't have fell like I did or at least I would have took me time, not been in such a hurry. I think it was a direct result of my bringing up at the Blind School. It had a bearing on me going for that girl because events proved that it was disastrous. The romance of the whole thing of course for a while it was heaven to me but then everything began to show. For instance she didn't come home one night, she was out all night. Eventually it got a lot worse. And well, the quarrels started, everything started. I went through hell.

Disabled young people who grew up outside institutions also experienced problems in forming intimate relationships. This problem was often rooted in a feeling that they were totally unattractive and sexually inadequate. The source of these anxieties was the sneering attitudes of the able-bodied and patronising representations of disabled people in popular culture. But when internalised by young disabled people themselves these feelings of sexual inferiority had a terrifying power. David Swift was a teenager in Nottingham in the late 1940s and early 1950s.

> I always thought that girls were doing me a favour by going out with me. I thought they didn't want someone like me walking on their arm. They couldn't show me off at home to their parents. So I was mostly out with the lads. I remember on one occasion we used to stand at the top of these shops and round the back of these shops was an entry. And my friend took this girl round there and he made love to her. I knew where he'd gone. Well anyway he brought her back and he said, 'It's

your turn now.' But I knew I couldn't do it. I couldn't do it standing up you see 'cos my legs wouldn't bend. I always wanted to make love to a girl but I just couldn't. There were several occasions when girls thought there was something wrong with me because I never did anything to them. I'd do all the kissing and smooching and what have you. But nothing else. I thought I'd never be able to make love. I felt inadequate all the time.

Irene Shelton was also a teenager in Nottingham at this time. At the age of eighteen she had to spend a year in a sanatorium after contracting TB. She experienced similar feelings of demoralisation about her sexual identity and marital prospects.

I was just eighteen. Tuberculosis was really horrible. It was something that people really dreaded getting, you know. So it was such a shock when I did go and have this x-ray and they said I was really ill. Both my lungs were full of tuberculosis. Well, I just cried for two days you know. And straight away I was in a sanatorium which changed my life completely, you know. You had such strange thoughts about tuberculosis you see, people were superstitious about it. Don't go anywhere near them. Even the doctors when I came out, they said, 'Well, if you're thinking of getting married try not to have children. It will probably be bad for you, you know. It might bring the TB back on again.' Then I had to go back every three months to the local doctors for visits, to check-ups. So I felt really bad about it. I felt it was something really difficult for me to cope with. I couldn't be sort of normal anymore. I couldn't be like the girl I used to be. I used to like dancing, I used to have friends. Now I wasn't able to go to work for a long time, I couldn't mix with people any more. I didn't think I'd get married. And I didn't think I'd have children.

Young disabled people often formed relationships with each other – or with those who were also in some way outsiders. Their understanding of each others feelings and problems often formed the basis for a deep love rooted in shared experience. David Swift met Irene in a youth club in dance in Nottingham in 1955.

I was playing table tennis and of course the ball fell into the corner and this girl picked it up and came to give it to me. I thought she was so beautiful. After that I couldn't bear to be alone without her. And to think I'd got her and nobody else had . . . I needed her, you know, because she was – she made me feel wonderful inside. She'd laugh and laugh and she'd never mention my legs at all, never. Never looked down on me one bit. And of course my mam and dad didn't want me to marry her because she'd been in a sanatorium. She'd had TB and of course everyone thought

Irene Shelton pictured at the age of seventeen in Nottingham in 1954.

you caught TB kissing – kiss someone with TB and you're going to swallow their lungs, 'cause they're coughing their lungs up. They said she would never be any good to me. 'Now just try to get out of it lad, – don't marry her.' But I wanted to be with her.

Many disabled people formed loving and intimate relationships which usually resulted in marriage. But such was the stigma of disability that this often involved overcoming opposition from the partner's family. Marriage to a disabled person was thought by the great majority of parents to be a most unsuitable match. Many couples battled against this prejudice and resisted their parents' attempts to interfere. But this background of arguments and ill-feeling often meant there was a great deal of tension during the wedding ceremony. For this was a public ritual in which it was very difficult to hide physical disabilities. Disabled brides or grooms felt themselves cruelly exposed and open to ridicule. David and Irene were married in 1956.

I wanted to come clean with Irene because she'd never ever made any point out of my disability. So I decided the night before we got married to come clean and be serious. And I sat her down, I said, 'I've got something to tell you. I've got bad legs, you know and I want you to know this before we get married.' I just felt as if I wanted her to know what she was letting herself in for. But of course she knew my legs were bad and I think we just laughed about it. But for days and days I'd been dreaming about the wedding. I was tripping up, frightened of tripping up on the old flagstones of the church floor. I had this fear of showing myself up. I was so embarrassed about being on show. And I knew that I wouldn't be able to put the ring on her finger because of my hands. I kept practising with two fingers and it kept twisting off. It was so thin and the gold was so slippy. I was so worried about showing Irene up.

David and Irene Swift's wedding day in 1956.
During weddings many disabled brides or
grooms felt themselves cruelly exposed and
open to ridicule.

But the next day me and my brother walked down to the church. I wanted to be there early because I didn't want anyone else to see me walking down the aisle. I was so nervous during the ceremony that I was going to drop the ring or fall over. How I got that ring on I don't know but I did. The worst was when we had to kneel in front of the vicar, I couldn't get up again properly.

And we walked back down the aisle together. I thought everybody was looking at my legs and I was conscious of that.

From the 1930s onwards the deaf community increasingly insisted on signing weddings for deaf people – and the church made some efforts to provide deaf parsons for these services. This meant that deaf couples were usually spared the potential embarrassment and humiliation of not being able to understand what was happening during the wedding ceremony. Instead deaf weddings often became joyous celebrations. Hazel and Dennis Boucher enjoyed a signing wedding when they were married in 1948.

Before we got married we had to go to the church for a practice for the ceremony. Things went fine. On the day itself I waited for Hazel to come and we went into the church. The parson we had was deaf himself. He could use his voice and talk but he was deaf. He signed and talked at the same time. It was better for us because we are deaf. We could understand what he was saying. If we'd had a hearing parson, we wouldn't have understood it. We would have been lost, so we were

Hazel and Dennis Boucher enjoyed a signing wedding when they were married in 1948.

pleased that we had a deaf parson to marry us. We had two deaf bridesmaids as well. Things ran smoothly, fine – everything went fine. We had about one hundred guests. And all the deaf guests were really pleased to see that we had a deaf parson to marry because they could follow the ceremony. For some of the guests its was the first signing wedding that they had been to and they really enjoyed it.

Facing a hostile world was often made easier when in a loving relationship. Marie Hagger married in 1948 at the age of twenty- three. Her husband Ernie, a sales representative, was very sensitive to her needs and they formed a close and mutually supportive relationship.

After we got married I felt as if I had someone I could always depend on. Because my husband understood that I was deaf and because it was never important to him he gave me a lot of confidence. He helped me and he became my ears really. If we were in a crowd of people and they were all talking he would tell me afterwards what they were all saying, fill me in on all the bits of gossip that I'd always missed before. So the times when I was with him gave me confidence for the times when I was on my own.

Marie Hagger married in 1948 at the age of 23. Her husband Ernie was very sensitive to her needs and they formed a close and mutually supportive relationship.

Marie and her husband pictured on holiday in Blackpool in 1949.

Mary Baker married in 1952 at the age of thirty. Her husband, Sidney, was an engineer. Together they overcame the hostility and prejudice with which they were confronted.

When I got married my husband helped me to get over the inferiority complex which I had. I used to worry in case I wasn't as good as other people and he used to say to me, 'You're as good as the next person. Take no notice of what they say.' Because when we were out walking people would stare at us sometimes, 'cause I had a high shoe. And I used to say, 'Well, I wonder if they've seen enough.' He said to ignore them and that they weren't worth bothering about and that I was as good as the rest of them. He was always telling me that so that my inferiority complex really disappeared and I just got on with him and we had a wonderful marriage.

Mary Baker married in 1952 at the age of 30. Together with her husband they overcame the hostility and prejudice with which they were confronted.

David and Irene Swift with their children. Family life was to bring much happiness to David and Irene.

The strong disapproval of disabled people having children which was reinforced by Eugenics ideas during the early part of the century continued, though in a diluted form, into the 1950s. The idea of disabled people coping and succeeding as parents was for example represented in fifties newsreels as something quite extraordinary. But some defied the prejudices of the time. For them parenthood was often especially fulfilling. David and Irene Swift have four children, three boys and a girl. David Swift:

> I felt great when Irene got pregnant. I felt real chuffed, you know. I told everyone. I wanted them to know, I wanted the world to know that I'd succeeded in being a father. I was that proud you know. Couldn't wait for her to put smocks on and to look pregnant. Because I was a dad, I was going to be a father. It was all working out, the idealisation of what I wanted, it was working. I'd got a beautiful woman, I'd got a baby and I was being loved for the first time. It was what I wanted. I felt that I could make love. I'd been told all through my teens that I was inadequate, that I'd never get married or have children. And our first baby made me feel – it fulfilled me. I felt one of the human race at last.

Betty Holland, who had polio, married a seaman in 1934.

> His mother was awful. She used to be really nasty to me and said that he shouldn't marry me because I wouldn't be able to make him a proper wife. I would never be able to manage a house or cook meals and keep him comfortable because of my disability. She really warned him off me but luckily for me we were dead set on the marriage and she couldn't stop us after all. And we managed perfectly. My husband used to help

me with things that I couldn't do and it all rolled along well for us. His mother was still horrible to me. She said that we would never be able to have children and that especially hurt me because I was hoping for a baby and I knew that my husband wanted to be a father. But I was determined to go on as if nothing was wrong and just hope that a baby would come. I was over the moon when I did get pregnant. And my little girl was all that we could have wished for.

For some the experience of parenthood and the creation of a family life of their own helped them forget the traumatic institutional experiences of their childhood. Mary Baker had three children.

I really enjoyed having the children. They were a great joy to me and my husband. And I felt as though I'd done a job worth doing. The little babies brought a lot of joy into our house. First Jim, then Alan and with Elaine our family was complete. I know we had our ups and downs but we managed to get through them and we brought the children up. It was a bit of a struggle but I managed them. Having my disability was very difficult really with three little ones but they were lovely and they were good kiddies. And I felt as if Halliwick was forgotten. I never mentioned

Mary Baker pictured with her husband and children. Family life helped her forget her appalling experience as a child at the Halliwick Home for Crippled Girls in the 1930s.

Halliwick to my husband. I blacked it out, forgot everything about it. I tried to put it to the back of my mind and it was a blank piece of paper so to speak. With the love of the children and my husband, and the little home that I ran, and doing their cooking, and having holidays with them and everything, I clean forgot about Halliwick.

Disabled people who brought up children outside of marriage often had to cope with additional problems and prejudices, such were the narrow social and sexual mores of the time. However, the joy of having a child often gave them strength to overcome hostile attitudes. Kathleen Turner was born in North London in 1930 with cerebral palsy. In 1953 at the age of twenty-three she had an illegitimate baby.

When I found out that I was pregnant I knew that I was breaking a taboo. I knew that lots of people and my family would be really shocked. I wasn't married and my boyfriend didn't want to marry me even when he knew that I was going to have his child. But none of this was in my mind as much as the feeling of pride and of happiness that I was having this baby. I felt as though I had really achieved something, something that was mine and that I would always have. I was in cloud cuckoo land. I never really thought that I wouldn't be able to cope or that my disability would make it difficult for me to have the child. Of course there was a lot of prejudice around then towards women who had babies and weren't married. I think it was especially harsh sometimes because of my disability. Some people just didn't believe that I would be able to have a baby and cope with bringing it up myself. But I just stood up for myself. The baby made me stronger. It gave me someone to love. When Chris my son was eventually born it was tinged with sadness because he wouldn't see his father but I wanted to keep him more than anything then. He made me feel independent, that I was as good as anyone else. I knew that I could bring my son up on my own and that's what I did.

Children could sometimes be very important assets in the struggle for survival often experienced by disabled single parent families. Ted Williams became a single parent when his wife left in 1939. He and his young son survived by forming a close working relationship.

The child's eyesight was a terrific help. For instance, if I wanted to go anywhere too difficult for the blind, well I'd know the way, the ins and outs but I wouldn't know how to negotiate them, but his eyesight, even at the age of four, young as he was, with the combination of the two of us we'd get to places where I couldn't get to otherwise. And as a result of this of course we drew closer together. I mean, whether the child knew I was dependent on him to that extent, I couldn't tell you, but I knew that I was. I always remember our favourite place. There's a woodyard in Sheffield and I was always one for messing around with wood. And so one of the favourites was to go to this yard with my son and because we couldn't afford to transport the wood back we used to carry it back with him hanging onto one end and me on the other. And he'd be shouting, which way we were to go. And that was for the best part of two miles. And in the home there were such things as peeling potatoes. I might not be sure that I'd got all the peel off them and so I'd show him and ask him if all the skin were off. He'd say, 'No there's some there dad.' And so on. He helped me in so many little ways. For instance one of my difficulties was cutting bread straight. I'd get the edge of a slice perhaps two inches thick and t'other half an inch and he used to help me and tell me to push the knife down a bit further and which way it should go.

But many who grew up in institutions during the first half of the century never escaped from them. They were to remain there all their lives. The effects of this policy of rigid segregation still exist today. Evelyn King remains in the mental handicap hospital where she was brought up. Her institutional life has deprived her of any opportunity to form a sexual relationship.

I didn't used to talk to the boys. It wasn't allowed. You would get into right bother if you even said one word to a boy then. So I used to be frightened of going near them. Didn't used to have any boyfriends in case you got punished by staff. You could get on the punishment villa for talking to boys. Some girls when they tried to speak to a boy, they got really punished. Some people would try to sneak letters to each other but they soon got stopped. I was always too scared, so I just kept right away from the boys.

Ted Williams pictured with his son Raymond. They formed a close working relationship which helped Ted to cope as a disabled single parent.

EPILOGUE

How does the experience of disability in Britain since the 1950s compare with that of the pre-war years? Although an answer to this question is strictly beyond the scope of this book we are concerned that many of the chilling and disturbing experiences we have documented may be taken as evidence that the pre-war treatment of disabled people was a kind of dark age from which we have now emerged. For many argue that there have been substantial improvements in the condition of disabled people with the coming of a more affluent society, the enjoyment of a higher standard of living by most families and the development of the welfare state. These social changes – so the argument goes – have led to a reduction in discrimination, exploitation and institutional abuse of disabled people. Thus it is often assumed that the experience of isolation, despair and powerlessness amongst disabled people – much in evidence, as we show, during the first half of the century – has been far less prevalent in recent decades. This is a very misleading and dangerous assumption – and, we hope, not the impression that our readers will carry away with them.

On the surface we appear to be a society that has much concern and compassion for disabled people. Charities bombard us with appeals to give money to help people whose lives have been 'tragically' struck by disability. Fund-raising for disabled people has now become a major entertainment event in the form of *Telethon* and *Children in Need* watched by millions on their television screens. However these appeals for the cash of the able-bodied viewers reinforce a passive and dependent image of disability. Disabled people are forced to play the role of beggars, albeit that they are often represented as 'heroic' and 'courageous' in coping with their 'personal tragedy'. The stage for the disabled beggar in the early years of the century was the street corner, now it is the television studio.

What this media circus reveals most of all is that attitudes towards disabled people have changed far less over the century than we often imagine. Disabled people are still denied the fundamental right to participate in society as equal citizens. Beneath the paternalism lies a deeply entrenched discrimination and exploitation. According to government figures disabled people are still today three times more likely to be out of work and unemployed for longer periods than non disabled people. When disabled men and women are given jobs in Britain in the 1990s they are normally unskilled and lowly paid. Disabled men in full time work earn a quarter less each week than non-disabled men working the same hours in the same job. Despite some improvements, most of our workplaces, our public buildings and our public transport system still present disabled people with major access problems.

Medical advances and improved living standards have reduced the extent of disabling diseases amongst children and young people through the course of the century. However these same changes have lengthened the life expectancy of older people amongst whom disability is now concentrated. There are now over six million disabled people in Britain of whom the majority are aged sixty or over. Many live in varying degrees of poverty and survive on welfare benefits. And the position of disabled children has not improved anywhere near as much as is popularly thought. There are for example periodic revelations of sexual abuse and violence towards disabled children and young people 'in care'. And although there has been legislation to encourage integrated schooling, there remain over 100,000 disabled children in special schools and institutions – a figure that has changed little since the 1970s.

In the last ten years there has been a growing awareness amongst disabled people that they have been – and still are – denied basic human rights. At the heart of this transformation in the understanding of the nature of disability has been the rise of the disability movement. This movement has in turn been driven by the emergence of a number of organisations controlled and run by disabled people themselves. The central concern of this movement is the individual and collective empowerment of disabled people. It challenges the dominant perception of disability as medical illness or personal tragedy and focuses instead on how society systematically handicaps disabled people. This new perspective also challenges the conventional wisdom that the history of disabled people in our century is one of general progress and improvement in their social condition. Histories written from this viewpoint should provide many new insights into the recent history of disabled people. We suspect that research into the experience of disability since the 1950s – about which remarkably little is known – may discover striking parallels with the experiences that we have documented earlier in the century. Certainly our conversations with younger disabled people suggest that they share much in common with those brought up before the last war. Patronising and hostile attitudes by the able-bodied and a refusal to recognise the rights of disabled people have shaped the experience of disability throughout the twentieth century.

FURTHER READING

Jo Campling, **Images of Ourselves: Women With Disabilities Talking**, Routledge, 1981.

Ted Cole, **Apart or A Part?: Integration and the Growth of British Special Education**, Open University Press, 1989.

Brian Grant, **The Deaf Advance: A History of the British Deaf Association**, Pentland Press, 1990.

John Hurt, **Outside the Mainstream: A History of Special Education**, Batsford, 1988.

Peter Jackson, **Britain's Deaf Heritage**, Pentland Press, 1990.

Michael Oliver, **The Politics of Disablement**, Macmillan Education, 1990.

Maggie Potts and Rebecca Fido, **A Fit Person To Be Removed: Personal Accounts of Life in a Mental Deficiency Institution**, Northcote House, 1991.

Patricia Potts, **Origins: Unit 9, Course E241 Special needs in Education**, Open University, 1982.

D. G. Pritchard, **Education and the Handicapped 1760–1960**, Routledge, 1963.

June Rose, **Changing Focus: The Development of Blind Welfare in Britain**, Hutchinson, 1970.

Oliver Sacks, **Seeing Voices**, Picador, 1990.

Paul Thompson, **The Voice of the Past: Oral History**, Oxford University Press, 1988.

Jerry White, **The Worst Street in North London: Campbell Bunk, Islington Between the Wars**, Routledge, 1986.

USEFUL CONTACTS

ORAL HISTORY:
Oral History Society, Department of Sociology, University of Essex, Wivenhoe Park, Colchester CO4 3SQ. Tel. 0206–873333.
Bob Perks, The Curator of Oral History, National Sound Archive, 28 Exhibition Road, London SW7 2AS. Tel. 071–589 6603.
Doc Rowe and Rosemary Dixon, London History Workshop Sound and Video Archive, 42 Queen Square, London WC1N 3AJ. Tel. 081–831 8871.

KEY ORGANISATIONS:
British Council of Organisations of Disabled People, De Bradelei House, Chapel Street, Belper, Derbyshire, DE5 1AR. Tel. 0773–828182.
British Polio Fellowship, Bell Close, Westend Road, Ryslip, Middlesex, HA4 6LP. Tel. 0895–675515.
Cerebral Palsy Helpline, Tel. 0800–626216.

Disability Alliance, First Floor East, Universal House, 88–94 Wentworth Street, London E1. Tel. 071–247 8776.
Greater London Association for Disabled People, 336 Brixton Road, London SW9 7AA. Tel. 071–274 0107.
National League of the Deaf/Blind, 18 Rainbow Court, Paston Ridings, Peterborough, PE4 6UP. Tel. 0733–73511.
Independent Living Fund, PO Box 183, Nottingham NG8 3RD. Tel. 0602–290423.
National Association of the Limbless Disabled, 31 The Mall, Ealing Broadway, London W5. Tel. 081–579 1758.
National League of the Blind and Disabled, 2 Tenterden Road, Tottenham, London N17 8BE. Tel. 081–808 6030.
Royal Association in Aid of the Deaf. 27 Old Oak Road, London W3. Tel. 081–743 6187.
Royal Association For Disability and Rehabilitation, 25 Mortimer Street, London W1. Tel. 071–637 5400.
Royal Institute for the Deaf, 135a High Street, London W3. Tel. 081–993 4748.
Royal National Institute for the Blind, 224 Great Portland Street, London W1N 6AA. Tel. 071–388 1266.
Royal National Institute for the Deaf, 105 Gower Street, London WC1. Tel. 071–387 8033.
The Spastics Society, 16 Fitzroy Square, London W1D 5HQ. Tel. 071–636 5020.

INDEX